NEVADA
TRIVIA

NEVADA TRIVIA

COMPILED BY KENNETH A. BOUTON & E. LYN BOUTON

Rutledge Hill Press®
Nashville, Tennessee

Published in Nashville, Tennessee, by Rutledge Hill Press, Inc., 211
Seventh Avenue North, Nashville, Tennessee 37219-1823. Distributed in
Canada by H. B. Fenn & Company, Ltd., 34 Nixon Road, Bolton, Ontario
L7E 1W2.

Typography by Roger A. DeLiso, Rutledge Hill Press®

Library of Congress Cataloging-in-Publication Data:
Bouton, Kenneth A., 1921–
    Nevada trivia / compiled by Kenneth A. Bouton and E. Lyn Bouton.
      p.   cm.
    ISBN 1-55853-730-9
    1. Nevada—Miscellanea.   2. Questions and answers.
    I. Bouton, E. Lyn.   II. Title.
    F841.6.B68   1999
    979.3—dc21   99-18326
                                     CIP

Printed in the United States of America
1 2 3 4 5 6 7 8 9—04 03 02 01 00 99

ACKNOWLEDGMENTS

The authors are grateful for the counsel and contributions of chambers of commerce throughout Nevada; to Frank Wright, curator of the Nevada State Museum in Las Vegas; to the Nellis Air Force Base public information office; to the Nevada Tourism Commission; to the Nevada Mining Association; to the Bechtel Corp.; to the Nevada Secretary of State; to Don Payne, for many years chief of the Las Vegas News Bureau; to Ted Quillin, historian of Las Vegas entertainment; to Las Vegas' longest-serving mayor, Oran K. Gragson; to Joe Cathcart, a Las Vegan who has walked the paths of pioneers in ghost towns throughout Nevada; to my daughter Marla who said "do it!" when she heard we were considering this project; and to all others whose profound interest in the study and preservation of the rich and colorful heritage of Nevada are reflected in these pages.

DEDICATION

To all who live in Nevada, whether under the neon glare of the glitz and glamour of its great cities, built on rolls of dice and hands dealt from a deck of cards, or on an isolated ranch in the shadow of a mountain, pock-marked by the hopes and dreams of early miners.

And to the millions of visitors from the world over who have helped establish Nevada as the place to play and have fun.

TABLE OF CONTENTS

PREFACE

Nevada is a land of contrast—stark and subtle. From snow-capped mountains to vast open stretches of the nation's largest desert, the Mohave. From its busy freeways to the "Loneliest Road in America." From its big cities, sparkling with miles of neon tubing and millions of lights, to the tiniest, most remote village, still clinging to its ghost-town heritage. From the fabulous Las Vegas Strip, with its gigantic re-creations of world-famous landmarks such as the Statue of Liberty and the Eiffel Tower, to main streets of still thriving rural towns that sprang up in the heartland of Nevada before the Civil War or Nevada statehood.

Nevada has tourist meccas in Laughlin and Las Vegas, the state's largest city and the "Entertainment Capital of the World." It has booming mining, ranching, and gambling towns which lie alongside I-80, and it has towns in central Nevada where remnants of old mines may outnumber the residents. It also has resorts at sparkling Lake Tahoe and the nearby cities of Carson City, Sparks, and Reno. No matter where one travels in this huge state, history joins hands with the twenty-first century around every bend in the road and over the next hill.

Nevada's rich and colorful history alone sets it apart from any other state in the nation. Her heritage and future have been recounted in scores of books. *Nevada Trivia* offers readers, in question-and-answer format, a unique thumbnail look at some of the people and events that have made Nevada number one in the hearts of visitors and residents alike.

The first question: Where did Nevada gets it name?
The first answer: *Nevada* means "snow-capped" in Spanish—the spectacular Sierra Nevada range forms part of the state's western boundary.

GEOGRAPHY

Q. What is the name of Nevada's largest man-made lake, shared by another state?

A. Lake Mead.

———∞∞∞———

Q. How and when was Lake Mead created?

A. By the construction of Hoover Dam on the Colorado River in the 1930s.

———∞∞∞———

Q. What is the name of Nevada's largest natural lake, shared by another state?

A. Lake Tahoe.

———∞∞∞———

Q. What is the largest natural lake wholly within Nevada?

A. Pyramid Lake, in western Nevada.

———∞∞∞———

Q. What is the name of Nevada's longest underground river?

A. The Amargosa.

Q. In what valley was cotton a staple crop, well into the 1970s?

A. The Amargosa Valley near the town of Pahrump, west of Las Vegas.

———∞∞∞———

Q. What is the name and elevation of Nevada's highest mountain?

A. Boundary Peak, on the western border, at 13,140 feet.

———∞∞∞———

Q. What is the name of Nevada's oldest and largest state park?

A. The Valley of Fire, about 50 miles northeast of Las Vegas.

———∞∞∞———

Q. What are the main geological features in the Valley of Fire?

A. Red sandstone and multihued spires, rocks, and monoliths.

———∞∞∞———

Q. What is the name of Nevada's only national park?

A. Great Basin National Park.

———∞∞∞———

Q. In what year did Congress establish this national park?

A. 1987.

———∞∞∞———

Q. What are the two main geological features in Great Basin National Park?

A. The Lehman Caves and Mt. Wheeler.

Q. What is the elevation of Mt. Wheeler, and how does it rank in elevation?

A. At 13,063 feet, Mt. Wheeler is the second highest mountain in Nevada.

───❦───

Q. Early discoveries of what three major ores led to boom towns, ghost towns, and permanent towns throughout northeastern Nevada?

A. Gold, silver, and copper.

───❦───

Q. Where in Nevada is one of the world's largest gold-producing regions?

A. In the Carlin (northern Nevada) area.

───❦───

Q. What river in northern Nevada lies along a part of what famed trail to the West?

A. The Humboldt River, on the Oregon Trail.

───❦───

Q. What river forms part of Nevada's eastern boundary with parts of Arizona and California?

A. The Colorado River.

───❦───

Q. How many dams on the Colorado River are on state boundary lines?

A. Two; Hoover Dam, on the Nevada-Arizona border, and Davis Dam, on the Arizona-California border.

Q. How long is the shoreline of Lake Mead?

A. More than 550 miles.

———❦———

Q. What is the name of Nevada's "newest" town?

A. Primm, at the tip of southern Nevada, on I-15.

———❦———

Q. Where did the town get its name?

A. For many years the tourist stop was known as Stateline. It was officially changed to Primm in 1998, named after the family that developed it.

———❦———

Q. A range of mountains in Nevada are often referred to as the Swiss Alps of America. What is the name and location of this range?

A. The Ruby Mountains in northern Nevada's Elko County region.

———❦———

Q. How many states border Nevada, and what are they?

A. Five: Arizona, California, Oregon, Idaho, and Utah.

———❦———

Q. Geographically, is Las Vegas located in a "valley"?

A. No. Las Vegas sits in a bowl, surrounded by mountains on all four sides.

Q. What is the name of the mountain range west of Las Vegas, and its highest peak?

A. The Spring Mountain Range; Mt. Charleston is its highest peak at 11,918 feet.

Q. What is the name of the mountain range north of Las Vegas?

A. The Sheep Mountain Range.

Q. What is the name of the mountain range east of Las Vegas?

A. The Frenchman.

Q. What is the name of the mountain range south of Las Vegas?

A. The McCullough Range.

Q. What is Nevada's largest city that lies farther west than Los Angeles?

A. Reno.

Q. Death Valley National Park lies just south of what Nevada town?

A. Beatty.

Q. What Nevada town on the Colorado River bears the name of its developer?

A. Laughlin, named after Don Laughlin, who began developing the area on the banks of the Colorado River in the late 1960s.

Q. What is the name of the large scenic area just west of Las Vegas?

A. The Red Rock Canyon National Recreation Area.

Q. What is the name of the refuge recently established near what southern Nevada town?

A. The Desert Tortoise Refuge is near Searchlight, at the southern tip of Nevada.

Q. What is the storage capacity of Lake Mead, formed by Hoover Dam?

A. 28,537,000 acre-feet.

Q. What geological feature is found just northwest of the town of Lovelock?

A. Giant tufa formations.

Q. What is the name of the national monument in the Amargosa Valley?

A. Devil's Hole, about 100 miles northwest of Las Vegas.

Q. What are the names and elevations of the tallest peaks in the Humboldt National Forest?

A. Hole in the Mountain, 11,027 feet; Humboldt Peak, 11,000 feet; Verdi Peak, 11,157 feet; Ruby Dome, 11,387 feet; and Pearl Peak, 10,847 feet.

Q. What percentage of Nevada land is owned by the federal government?

A. About 87 percent.

Q. What Nevada county is home to more than half the state's population?

A. Clark County (which includes the city of Las Vegas).

Q. Where are Nevada's Hot Springs Mountains?

A. Along I-80 in western Nevada.

Q. What famed geological feature is near the town of Beowawe?

A. The Beowawe Geysers.

Q. What is the total land area of Nevada?

A. 110,540 square miles.

Q. How does Nevada rank in size with all other states?

A. Seventh.

Q. What is the land area of Nye County?

A. 18,064 square miles.

Q. What is Nevada's smallest county, and that county's area in square miles?

A. Carson City County, 153 square miles.

───❦───

Q. What is the name and land area of Nevada's second largest county?

A. Elko County, in northern Nevada, contains 17,181 square miles.

───❦───

Q. What mountain range separates much of Nevada from California?

A. The Sierra Nevada Range.

───❦───

Q. In what geographical region is Las Vegas and much of southern Nevada located?

A. The Mohave Desert.

───❦───

Q. What southern Nevada area grows grapes and has its own winery?

A. The Pahrump Valley, about an hour west of Las Vegas.

───❦───

Q. A large area north of Las Vegas is noted for what geological feature?

A. Its natural warm springs, west of Glendale on S.R. 168.

Q. What geological feature led to the first development of Las Vegas?

A. An abundance of water from springs and artesian wells.

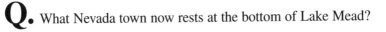

Q. What Nevada town now rests at the bottom of Lake Mead?

A. St. Thomas, a small community northeast of Las Vegas, had to be abandoned when Lake Mead was created.

Q. Where is the geographic center of Nevada?

A. In Lander County, about ten miles south of U.S. Hwy. 50 and midway between the towns of Eureka and Austin.

Q. Great Basin National Park is wholly within Nevada; what other national park extends into Nevada?

A. A small section of Death Valley National Park is in Nye County, Nevada.

Q. What towns are at the west and east ends of I-80 in Nevada?

A. West Verdi at the California border and West Wendover at the Utah state line.

Q. What town is near the southern tip of Nevada, and what is its elevation?

A. Laughlin, on the banks of the Colorado River, is 535 feet above sea level.

Q. What major gold-producing area is just south of Battle Mountain?

A. Copper Canyon.

Q. What highway parallels the Pony Express route across Nevada?

A. U.S. 50.

Q. What is the name of the nation's largest historic district?

A. The Comstock District, in western Nevada.

Q. What Nevada town claims to be the state's first settlement?

A. Dayton, settled in 1849.

Q. Where did the town of Dayton get its name?

A. In 1861, John Day surveyed the town's boundaries, and for his work, the settlement was named Day Town, later to become Dayton.

Q. Where and when was the first recorded discovery of gold in Nevada?

A. In Gold Canyon near present-day Dayton, in 1849.

Q. How many mountains in Nevada are over 9,000 feet high?

A. Fifty-one.

Q. What are the highest and lowest elevations in Nevada?

A. 13,145 feet and 470 feet.

Q. Nevada is generally situated in what geographic area of the world?

A. The Great Basin of the North American Continent.

Q. What is the elevation of Mt. Charleston, just west of Las Vegas?

A. 11,918 feet.

Q. What is Nevada's longest river?

A. The Humboldt River, which meanders 500 miles from the Humboldt Mountains east of Elko to the Humboldt Sink, south of Lovelock.

Q. What are the names and sizes of Nevada's two national forests?

A. Toiyabe and Humboldt; each contains about two-and-a-half million acres, divided into 19 forest areas.

Q. What is the name of the large geological formation in the Amargosa Valley?

A. The Amargosa Sand Dunes, clearly visible from U.S. Hwy. 95.

Q. What is a common geological feature of Spring Valley State Park and Echo Canyon State Recreation Area?

A. Both sites contain 65-acre reservoirs.

Q. What mountain range in Nevada is the wettest and therefore most verdant?

A. The Ruby Mountains in northern Nevada.

Q. What highway goes over Nevada's highest mountain pass?

A. The Mt. Rose Highway, S.R. 431, south of Reno, climbs to 8,911 feet.

Q. How much higher in elevation is Lake Tahoe than the town of Carson City, about nine miles away by air?

A. The lake is nearly 1,500 feet higher.

Q. Some of Nevada's highest mountains are in mountain ranges near Austin. Name two that are over 11,000 feet in elevation.

A. Bunker Hill, 11,474 feet, and Mt. Jefferson, 11,807 feet.

Q. What is the name and general location of Nevada's second longest river?

A. The Reese River in central Nevada.

Q. Austin is built on the steep sides of what canyon?

A. Pony Canyon.

Q. In its heyday in the 1870s, how many people lived in Austin and in the Pony Canyon area?

A. About 10,000.

Q. Traveling from west to east across Nevada, what is the name of the first of three great valleys that lie in the heart of Nevada?

A. The Reese River Valley.

———❧———

Q. What are the names of the other two major valleys in central Nevada?

A. Big Smoky Valley, the largest of the three, and Monitor Valley, both east of Austin.

———❧———

Q. What is the only natural outlet for treated sewage and runoff water from the Las Vegas Valley?

A. The Las Vegas Wash.

———❧———

Q. Into what body of water does the Las Vegas Wash dump?

A. Lake Mead and the Colorado River.

———❧———

Q. The Las Vegas Valley (or bowl) slopes down in what direction?

A. East.

———❧———

Q. What is the mountain on the east side of the Las Vegas Valley commonly called?

A. Sunrise Mountain.

———❧———

Q. What mineral abounds in the Las Vegas area and is mined extensively?

A. Gypsum.

Q. What is the main product manufactured in the Las Vegas area from gypsum?

A. Wallboard, or "plaster board."

Q. What is the smallest incorporated town in Nevada?

A. Gabbs, east of Hawthorne, population 660.

Q. What is Nevada's official state rock?

A. Sandstone.

Q. What is the average annual statewide precipitation?

A. Nine inches.

Q. Where in Nevada can you find a glacier?

A. Great Basin National Park.

Q. What is the size of Nevada's largest and oldest state park?

A. The Valley of Fire, which contains 34,880 acres.

Q. Along with its spectacular sandstone spires and many petroglyphs, what other geological feature is found in the Valley of Fire?

A. Areas of petrified wood.

Q. What Nevada city was the home of "Tahoe Beer" for over a century?

A. Carson City.

———

Q. The Atlantic Cable was financed by Nevada mining money from what area?

A. Virginia City and the Comstock Lode.

———

Q. By 1915, how many miles of railroad tracks were there in Nevada?

A. About 2,000.

———

Q. What happened on the south flank of Nevada's Sun Mountain in 1859?

A. Gold was discovered.

———

Q. In 1859, how many non–Native Americans lived in what would become Nevada?

A. Less than 300.

———

Q. How many farms and ranches were there in Nevada by the early 1980s?

A. Twenty-seven hundred.

———

Q. What was the average size of these farms and ranches?

A. 3,296 acres, or more than five square miles.

Q. What is the total acreage of farm and grazing land in Nevada?

A. Estimated at nine million acres.

Q. Vast areas in Nevada produce what form of energy?

A. Geothermal.

Q. In 1982 alone, how many leases for geothermal energy sources were issued?

A. Eight hundred.

Q. In 1982, how many major companies were drilling for oil in eastern Nevada?

A. Seven.

Q. How many major oil fields are currently producing in eastern Nevada?

A. Three.

Q. Studies and preliminary developments for what other form of energy abound in Nevada?

A. Solar energy.

Q. What is the altitude at Austin, near the center of Nevada?

A. 6,600 feet.

Q. Austin was a key point on what pioneer mail route?

A. The Pony Express.

Q. In its early history, Lander County occupied how much of what is now Nevada?

A. About one-third.

Q. In what year was uranium discovered in the Reese River Mining District?

A. 1953.

Q. What Nevada town is considered one of the most remote in the state?

A. Austin.

Q. What are the closest towns to Austin in all directions?

A. Fallon is 110 miles west; Battle Mountain is 70 miles north; Eureka is 70 miles east; and Tonopah is 117 miles south.

Q. The discovery of silver ore near Austin by William Talcott in 1862 did what?

A. It started a silver boom second only to the Comstock ore finds.

Q. Austin grew out of what other two mining settlements nearby?

A. Jacobsville and Clifton.

Q. How large is the Reno metropolitan statistical area (Washoe County)?

A. 6,608 square miles.

Q. What is the elevation of the Reno metro area?

A. 4,500 feet above sea level.

Q. State official Dean Judson does what very important task each November?

A. As state demographer, he annually estimates the population of Nevada's cities, counties, and unincorporated areas.

Q. Of what importance are these annual population estimates?

A. They are used by the Nevada Dept. of Taxation to allocate liquor, cigarette, and other taxes to the various jurisdictions.

Q. What is a function of the state engineer that is crucial to all Nevadans?

A. The state engineer decides when, where—and if—water wells can be drilled.

Q. Who were the two former state engineers who became governors of Nevada?

A. Emmett Boyle (1915–23) and James Scrugham (1923–27).

Q. What is the name of the famed northern Nevada ranch in Elko County that was purchased in December 1989 by a California car dealer?

A. The PX Ranch.

Q. What was the price paid for the PX Ranch?

A. A reported $5 million.

Q. Where is one of Nevada's largest thermal energy projects?

A. The Beowawe Geysers in northern Nevada.

Q. In what Nevada area is wine now produced instead of cotton?

A. The Pahrump Valley.

Q. In what area was cotton "the king of crops" for many years?

A. Pahrump, which had its own cotton gin during the mid-1900s.

Q. What is the elevation of Tonopah?

A. 6,020 feet above sea level.

Q. Tonopah sits on top of how many miles of mining tunnels?

A. About 100.

Q. Where is Nevada's scenic Peavine Canyon?

A. About 54 miles north of Tonopah.

Q. What is the name of the mountain peak that is a backdrop for Tonopah?

A. Lone Mountain.

Q. What occupies the site of Jim Butler's original mining claim in Tonopah?

A. The Tonopah Mining Park Project.

Q. What Nevada town was known as the Queen of the Silver Camps?

A. Tonopah.

Q. What is the name of Nevada's "almost a ghost town," where many open-pit gold mines still operate?

A. Manhattan.

Q. Gold and silver properties that were once part of the mining empire of Howard Hughes are where?

A. Manhattan.

Q. Where did Nevada's Walker River get its name?

A. It was named by explorer John Fremont in honor of a member of his party that camped on the river west of Yerington on January 21, 1844.

Q. By what name was the town of Yerington first known?

A. Greenfield.

⊸⊸⊸

Q. Where did Yerington get its name?

A. It was named for Henry Marvin Yerington, who settlers hoped would bring the railroad into town.

⊸⊸⊸

Q. Yerington is in what famed agricultural valley?

A. The Mason Valley.

⊸⊸⊸

Q. What was a major industry in the town of Weed Heights from 1952 to 1978?

A. Copper mining.

⊸⊸⊸

Q. The Yerington–Weed Heights area was known as what?

A. The Cattle Kingdom in the Copper Hills.

⊸⊸⊸

Q. Lyon County produces what percentage of Nevada's agricultural products?

A. Twenty-three percent.

⊸⊸⊸

Q. Yerington, the county seat of Lyon County, was incorporated in what year?

A. 1907.

Q. How much land in Nevada is forested?

A. About 12,000 square miles.

———∞∞∞———

Q. What was an early name for the town of Dayton?

A. Chinatown.

———∞∞∞———

Q. Chinatown became what before it was named Dayton?

A. Nevada City.

———∞∞∞———

Q. Where did Susan's Bluff get its name?

A. It was named for an immigrant who was buried at the foot of the bluff.

———∞∞∞———

Q. What is the name of the rugged gorge where Lyon and Story Counties meet?

A. Devil's Gate.

———∞∞∞———

Q. How did the old mining town of Como get its name?

A. According to legend, it was named by a homesick Italian miner.

———∞∞∞———

Q. When and where did Fort Churchill get its name?

A. It was named in 1860 for Gen. Sylvester Churchill, U.S. army inspector general.

Q. Where is Ragtown Pass, an early wagon road?

A. On U.S. Hwy. 50A, at the eastern edge of Lyon County.

Q. What and where was Coffin's Station?

A. A toll road through Fernley's Valley, run by James Coffin and his two brothers.

Q. Where did the Truckee River get its name?

A. Most records say the river was named for Captain Truckee, a northern Paiute leader and guide.

Q. Where was the Talapoosa Mining District, and how did it get its name?

A. About 12 miles south of Fernley; the name came from the Talapoosa River in Alabama.

Q. What is the origin of the name Wabuska, in Lyon County?

A. The name is believed to mean "white grass" or "vegetation" in the dialect of Washoe Indians.

Q. Where was the area known as Little Desert or Ten-Mile Desert?

A. West of the town of Dayton.

Q. Where was the Twelve-Mile Desert?

A. An area east of the town of Dayton.

Q. What area is known as Nevada's Garden Spot?

A. The Mason Valley.

Q. How many Nevada counties border on the state of California?

A. Eight.

Q. What county in Nevada—one of the largest in the nation—borders on California?

A. Nye County.

Q. How many Nevada counties border on Utah?

A. Four.

Q. Where did the town of Weed Heights get its name?

A. Then a company town, it was named after Clyde E. Weed, chairman of the board of the Anaconda Company.

Q. Where was the first major copper operation brought into production after World War II?

A. The Anaconda Company's Yerington mine and plant.

Q. What was the annual copper production schedule of this plant?

A. Seventy-five million pounds.

Q. In addition to copper, Anaconda was a leading producer of what other minerals from its Yerington–Weed Heights mines?

A. Uranium, aluminum, lead, and zinc.

Q. What other precious metals were by-products of those mines?

A. Gold, silver, and platinum.

Q. What town first served as the seat of Lyon County?

A. Dayton.

Q. In what year did Dayton get electrical power?

A. 1905.

Q. When was the Fernley railroad station listed in the official railroad guide?

A. January 1905.

Q. What was the name of Fernley's earliest railroad line?

A. The Fernley-Lassen Line.

Q. When was the Fernley depot closed by the Southern Pacific Railroad?

A. September 1985.

Q. What Nevada town is at the west end of the historic 40-Mile Desert?

A. Fernley.

Q. What were two major objectives for immigrants crossing this desert?

A. To reach Boiling Springs (now Brady's Hot Springs), and the Truckee River.

Q. What was the 40-Mile Desert in prehistoric times?

A. Most of it was ancient Lake Lahontan.

Q. Who discovered the Lehman Caves, and when?

A. Absalom Lehman, a local rancher and miner, discovered them in 1885.

Q. With a population of 10 to 20, where is the town of Hooterville?

A. Off the Pyramid Lake Highway, just northeast of Wadsworth.

Q. Where is Sand Mountain, also called Singing Sand Mountain?

A. About 30 miles east of Fallon, on U.S. Hwy. 50.

Q. How did this mountain get its name?

A. Wind moving over the 600-foot-high sand dune creates "music."

Q. How many "singing" dunes are there in North America, according to geologists?

A. Only three.

———— ∞∞∞ ————

Q. Where is Bailey's Hot Springs resort?

A. About three miles north of Beatty on U.S. Hwy. 95.

———— ∞∞∞ ————

Q. When did construction start on the Sutro Tunnel to drain water from the Comstock Lode?

A. October 19, 1869.

———— ∞∞∞ ————

Q. How much did it cost to build the approximately 4-mile-long tunnel?

A. $4.5 million.

———— ∞∞∞ ————

Q. How did the town of Lovelock gets its name?

A. It was so named by the Central Pacific Railroad to honor George Lovelock, who in 1867 donated 85 acres for a townsite, railroad right-of-way, and depot.

———— ∞∞∞ ————

Q. What cave in Nevada is listed in the National Register of Historic Places?

A. Lovelock Cave.

Q. What is the name for geological formations found in many areas in Nevada that are created by hot water rising out of the ground?

A. Tufas.

———— ∞∞∞ ————

Q. Tufa formations ranging up to 20 feet high and spread out over 100 acres are found just northwest of what Nevada town?

A. Lovelock.

———— ∞∞∞ ————

Q. What is the name of the famed historical river that runs through Lovelock?

A. The Humboldt.

———— ∞∞∞ ————

Q. What is the name of a flood control and irrigation project on the Humboldt River north of Lovelock, and when was it built?

A. The Rye Patch Dam and Reservoir, north of Lovelock, was built in 1935–36.

———— ∞∞∞ ————

Q. What is the storage capacity and the length of the reservoir?

A. 179,000 acre-feet can be stored in the 22-mile-long lake behind the dam.

———— ∞∞∞ ————

Q. Where did the name Rye Patch come from?

A. A mining town in the 1860s; it got its name from wild rye growing nearby.

Q. Where is Troy Canyon, and for what is it noted?

A. Northeast of Lovelock, the canyon is noted for its fossil deposits.

Q. In what county are what may be Nevada's best rockhounding areas?

A. Pershing County.

Q. What other geological features can be seen in this same area?

A. Earthquake faults.

Q. How did the town of Pahrump get its name?

A. Paiute Indians named the valley Pah, meaning "water," and Rimpi, meaning "stone" or "rock." Pah Rimpi later became Pahrump.

Q. Pahrump makes what claim for its growth?

A. That it is the fastest-growing rural town in America.

Q. What has been the growth rate of Pahrump for the past seven years?

A. Fifteen to seventeen percent.

Q. Pahrump is a gateway to what national park?

A. Death Valley.

Q. Though Nevada became a state in 1864, until 1867 much of what is now southern Nevada was part of what jurisdiction?

A. The Arizona Territory.

———∞∞∞———

Q. What is the name of the Paiute Indian chief who once lived in Pahrump?

A. Chief Tecopa, who died there in 1904.

———∞∞∞———

Q. When was the first paved road built between Pahrump and Las Vegas?

A. 1954.

———∞∞∞———

Q. Where is Cathedral Canyon?

A. About 20 miles southeast of Pahrump, off the Tecopa (CA) Highway.

———∞∞∞———

Q. What are the main features of Cathedral Canyon?

A. The natural canyon features a pedestrian suspension bridge, walking paths, colorful tapestries, nativity scenes, a statue of Christ, stained glass, and other items with a religious theme.

———∞∞∞———

Q. Who developed Cathedral Canyon?

A. The late Roland Wiley, whose Hidden Hills Ranch includes the canyon.

Q. Where is southern Nevada's only developed winter sports area?

A. On 11,918-foot Mt. Charleston, 35 miles northwest of Las Vegas.

Q. What are the names of the major developed areas on Mt. Charleston?

A. Lee and Kyle Canyons, which offer year-round recreation opportunities.

Q. In addition to its towering red sandstone, what is another main attraction in the Red Rock Canyon?

A. A 13-mile, one-way, scenic drive.

Q. Under what Nevada town were many tunnels built, but for non-mining uses?

A. Eureka.

Q. The tunnels (now inoperable) were built for what purpose?

A. The tunnels connected what in the old days were breweries so that deliveries to the town's many saloons could be made despite inclement weather.

Q. The largest-ever gold nugget was found where in Nevada?

A. A 25-pound nugget, valued at $6,000, was found near the old mining camp of Osceola.

Q. Famed for its placer mining, Osceola is said to be the longest-lived placer camp in Nevada. During what years was this camp in operation?

A. 1872 to 1940.

Q. A canyon and mountain range in White Pine County are named for what officer who helped establish the Pony Express route through this area?

A. Maj. Howard E. Egan.

Q. For whom was Nevada's Steptoe Valley named?

A. Col. E. J. Steptoe, a famed Old West Indian fighter.

Q. How did the town of Hawthorne get its name?

A. It was named for W. A. Hawthorn, contractor for a new wagon road in the area.

Q. On what date were townsite lots auctioned off in Hawthorne?

A. April 14, 1881.

Q. What was the average price paid for Hawthorne townsite lots?

A. About $112.

Q. From 1878 to 1883, the two 20-stamp mills in Bonneville processed how much ore a day?

A. Up to 120 tons.

Q. Walker Lake is one of only three places in Nevada where what form of transportation played a role in the state's early transportation system?

A. Steamboats.

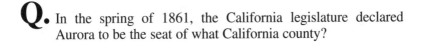

Q. What was the name of the company that operated on Walker Lake?

A. The Walker Lake Navigation Company.

Q. In the early 1860s, what town was claimed by both Nevada Territory and California?

A. Aurora.

Q. In the spring of 1861, the California legislature declared Aurora to be the seat of what California county?

A. The newly created Mono County.

Q. In November of 1861, Nevada declared Aurora to be the seat of what Nevada county?

A. Esmeralda.

Q. How long did this double-county-seat status last?

A. Nearly two years.

Q. Who paid for the $3.5 million bridge across the Colorado River that links Bullhead City, AZ, and Laughlin, NV?

A. Don Laughlin, who founded the river resort town that bears his name.

———❧———

Q. A U.S. Post Office is located in what hotel/casino in Nevada?

A. The Riverside, in Laughlin.

———❧———

Q. Who decided that the town of Laughlin should be named after its founder?

A. A U.S. Postal Service inspector, who in 1968 insisted the town have a name for delivery of mail.

———❧———

Q. What governmental feature distinguishes Laughlin from Nevada's other major resort towns?

A. It is the largest town that is unincorporated.

———❧———

Q. Who owns and operates the only Native American–owned casino in Nevada?

A. The Fort Mojave Indian Tribe owns the Avi, located 12 miles downriver from Laughlin.

———❧———

Q. What does the word "Avi" mean in the Mojave tribal language?

A. "Money" or "loose change."

ENTERTAINMENT

C H A P T E R   T W O

Q. In 1970, Las Vegas Mayor *pro tem* Hank Thornley presented a Proclamation of Appreciation to what entertainer who appeared at the Frontier Hotel?

A. Frank Sinatra Jr.

Q. Who was one of the Frontier Hotel's most popular attractions in 1970?

A. Bob Newhart.

Q. What famous singing group performed at the Frontier in the 1970s?

A. Diana Ross and the Supremes.

Q. When and where was the Second Annual Howard Hughes Invitational Tennis Championship held?

A. At the Frontier Hotel in Las Vegas, May 13–17, 1970.

Q. Six Las Vegas hotels, the Landmark, the Desert Inn, the Frontier, the Castaways, the Sands, and the Silver Slipper, were all owned by a world-famous billionaire in the early 1970s. Who was he?

A. Howard Hughes.

Q. What was the name of the first major gambling resort hotel on the Las Vegas Strip; it was destroyed by fire in June 1960?

A. The El Rancho Vegas.

Q. In what town did "big name" entertainment in casinos begin?

A. Elko.

Q. What is the name of Nevada's first hotel/casino to use "big name" entertainers to draw customers?

A. The Commercial Hotel in Elko.

Q. What famed entertainer at one time owned several ranching properties north of Elko?

A. Bing Crosby.

Q. Who were two other big name entertainers to become "ranchers" in the Elko area in the 1940s?

A. Joel McRae and Jimmy Stewart.

Q. What hotel and bar in Elko has been in continuous operation since 1915?

A. The Clifton.

Q. Who was the pioneer operator of hotels and saloons in many Nevada towns who in 1925 bought the Commercial Hotel in Elko?

A. Newton Crumley.

Q. Who was one of the first "big name" entertainers to appear at the Commercial Hotel?

A. Ted Lewis and his 21-person orchestra had an 8-day engagement in 1941.

———— ∞∞∞ ————

Q. What is the name of Elko's main commercial street?

A. Idaho Street, which was once U.S. Hwy. 40.

———— ∞∞∞ ————

Q. The nationally famed annual Cowboy Poetry Gathering is held where?

A. At the Western Folklife Center in Elko.

———— ∞∞∞ ————

Q. What other major celebration is Elko noted for?

A. The annual Basque Festival.

———— ∞∞∞ ————

Q. Who was the Elko saddlemaker whose American Eagle model won gold awards at the 1904 St. Louis World's Fair and the 1905 Lewis and Clark Exposition in Portland?

A. G. S. Garcia, who came to Elko in 1896.

———— ∞∞∞ ————

Q. A group of Hollywood stars who appeared regularly in Las Vegas during the 1960s and 1970s were known by what name?

A. The Rat Pack.

Q. Who were the members of the Rat Pack?

A. Frank Sinatra, Dean Martin, Joey Bishop, Sammy Davis Jr., and Peter Lawford.

Q. At what hotel (no longer in existence) did they appear?

A. The Sands.

Q. How many famed Las Vegas hotels were imploded in the 1990s to make way for the construction of new, mega-resort developments?

A. Four: the Dunes, the Landmark Tower, the Hacienda, and the Aladdin.

Q. What famous singer got his start in what downtown Las Vegas hotel?

A. Wayne Newton, who appeared in the 1950s with his brother Jerry at the Fremont.

Q. What was the original name of what is now the Las Vegas Hilton Hotel?

A. The International.

Q. Who was the famous movie actress who died in a plane crash on a mountain just southwest of Las Vegas (and in what year)?

A. Carole Lombard died in 1942 in a crash on Mt. Potosi.

Q. How many miles of neon tubing are there in Las Vegas signs?

A. Estimated at more than 15,000 miles.

———— ∞∞∞ ————

Q. What famous Las Vegas event was once ranked third of its kind in the nation?

A. The Elks annual Helldorado Parade.

———— ∞∞∞ ————

Q. What landmark Las Vegas Strip hotel was built by a reputed gangland figure?

A. The original Flamingo Hotel was built by Benjamin "Bugsy" Siegel.

———— ∞∞∞ ————

Q. In what year was the Flamingo completed?

A. In 1946.

———— ∞∞∞ ————

Q. Name three stars who were among early performers at the Flamingo Hotel.

A. Rose Marie, Kay Starr, and Jimmy Durante.

———— ∞∞∞ ————

Q. Who were the first black entertainers to perform in Las Vegas?

A. The Mills Brothers.

———— ∞∞∞ ————

Q. What was the most significant change in Nevada's gaming and entertainment industry in the 1960s?

A. The end of mob ownership of many hotels, when they were acquired by corporations.

Q. What U.S. President made his only nightclub appearance in Las Vegas?

A. Ronald Reagan.

Q. In what hotel did Reagan appear, and what did his act feature?

A. The New Frontier Hotel, where he was on stage with trained chimpanzees.

Q. Who was the comedian who starred at the New Frontier in 1956, and what singer opened his show?

A. Shecky Greene, whose opening act was Elvis Presley.

Q. In November of 1950, a U.S. senator from Tennessee tried to "shut down" Las Vegas. Who was he, and what congressional committee did he chair?

A. Estes Kefauver, head of the House Un-American Activities Committee.

Q. Who was the leading star at the Riviera Hotel for many years?

A. Pianist and entertainer Liberace.

Q. Who were the three members of a famous entertainment family who appeared in Las Vegas during the 1970s?

A. Singers Frank Sinatra, Frank Sinatra Jr., and Nancy Sinatra.

Q. What was the first estimated cost to build the Flamingo Hotel and the final cost, by the time the hotel opened in 1946?

A. Original construction costs, pegged at $1 million, increased to $6 million.

Q. What was the first high-rise hotel/casino built in downtown Las Vegas?

A. The Fremont Hotel, built in the 1950s.

Q. How many tourists came to the Las Vegas area in 1995?

A. Some 30 million, according to the Las Vegas Visitors and Convention Authority.

Q. What were three major events in 1931 that had a special impact on Las Vegas and helped boost the growth and prosperity of the entire state?

A. The start of construction of the Hoover Dam on the nearby Colorado River, actions by the state legislature to legalize casino-style gambling, and the establishment of a six-week residency for divorces.

Q. Fremont Street in downtown Las Vegas is also known by what slang term?

A. Glitter Gulch.

Q. What is the most famous attraction in downtown Las Vegas?

A. The Fremont Street Experience, where millions of colored lights in an overhead canopy and a huge sound system create spectacular shows.

Q. In the 1960s, what was the tallest structure in downtown Las Vegas?

A. The Mint Hotel (which is now part of the Horseshoe Club).

Q. What hotel in downtown Las Vegas now occupies the site of the old Union Pacific Railroad depot?

A. Jackie Gaughn's Plaza Hotel and Casino, also called the Union Plaza.

Q. On February 15, 1954, what Hollywood (and later, Washington, D.C.) celebrity began a two-week engagement at what Las Vegas Strip hotel?

A. Ronald Reagan, billed as a "singer and dancer," opened at the Last Frontier.

Q. On what date did entertainer Elvis Presley make a triumphant return to Las Vegas, after his unsuccessful debut 13 years earlier?

A. July 31, 1969.

Q. Where is the annual Pizen Switch Roundup held?

A. Yerington.

Q. Where is the locale for the Uptown Downtown ARTown Festival?

A. Reno.

Q. What band backed Frank Sinatra in his early appearances at the Sands Hotel?

A. Count Basie and his orchestra.

———◇◇◇———

Q. When did the Royal Nevada Hotel/Casino open on the Las Vegas Strip?

A. May 1955.

———◇◇◇———

Q. What other Strip hotels/casinos opened during this period?

A. The Riviera and the Dunes.

———◇◇◇———

Q. Who starred at the Riviera's grand opening?

A. Liberace.

———◇◇◇———

Q. What city hosts the annual Nevada State Fair?

A. Reno.

———◇◇◇———

Q. In what Nevada town are the International Camel Races?

A. Virginia City.

———◇◇◇———

Q. Who were the first entertainers at the Meadows Club?

A. The Meadowlarks.

Q. What was the name of the club opened by Guy McAfee in the 1930s?

A. The Paradise Club, on old U.S. Hwy. 91.

Q. What was the first luxury hotel/casino in downtown Las Vegas?

A. The Apache Hotel, a three-story hotel with about 100 rooms.

Q. In what year was the first convention held in Las Vegas?

A. 1935.

Q. What group came to Las Vegas for the town's first convention?

A. A Shriners group from Los Angeles.

Q. In what year did the Las Vegas Helldorado Days begin?

A. 1935.

Q. What organization founded this annual festival?

A. The Las Vegas Elks Lodge.

Q. What is Helldorado Days?

A. A week-long festival highlighted by parades, to keep Las Vegas' frontier heritage alive.

Q. What was the first hotel/casino on the Las Vegas Strip, who built it, and in what year?

A. Tommy Hull built the El Rancho Vegas in 1941.

Q. The El Rancho Vegas is credited with what phase in the entertainment industry?

A. It was the start of resort development in the Las Vegas area.

Q. Who was the comedian/host at the El Rancho?

A. Joe E. Lewis.

Q. Who were some of the invited stars introduced by Lewis?

A. Loretta Young, Milton Berle, Jackie Gleason, Jimmy Durante, "Hoot" Gibson, Nat King Cole, and Glen Ford.

Q. Who made their debut in Las Vegas at the Nevada Biltmore?

A. Don, Harry, and Herb, the Mills Brothers.

Q. Who were other headliners at the Nevada Biltmore?

A. Martha Raye, and Bud Abbot and Lou Costello.

Q. What Nevada hotel/casino has one of the world's tallest and fastest roller coasters?

A. Buffalo Bill's Hotel/Casino, in Primm, houses the Desperado.

Q. How high is the coaster's first drop, and at what speed does it travel?

A. The first drop is 225 feet, and the coaster travels at nearly 90 miles an hour!

———∞∞———

Q. Name two hotel/casinos on the Las Vegas Strip whose names are repeated?

A. Circus Circus, and New York–New York.

———∞∞———

Q. What famous New York harbor landmark is recreated in miniature at New York–New York?

A. The Statue of Liberty.

———∞∞———

Q. What Las Vegas Strip hotel has an enclosed roller coaster?

A. Circus Circus.

———∞∞———

Q. A replica of an active volcano is an outdoor attraction at what Las Vegas Strip hotel/casino?

A. Steve Wynn's Mirage Hotel.

———∞∞———

Q. What was the name of the second hotel/casino built on the Las Vegas Strip?

A. The Last Frontier.

Q. What major change in entertainment did The Last Frontier introduce?

A. The so-called star policy, where "name" entertainers performed.

━━━ ❧ ━━━

Q. Who was the first "name" entertainer at The Last Frontier?

A. Sophie Tucker, who performed in the Opera House showroom.

━━━ ❧ ━━━

Q. What other major project was done by The Last Frontier to keep alive the traditions of the Old West?

A. The hotel built a western village behind the adjacent Silver Slipper gambling hall.

━━━ ❧ ━━━

Q. Where on the Las Vegas Strip was the Little Church of the West?

A. On the grounds of The Last Frontier Hotel.

━━━ ❧ ━━━

Q. What musical group played from midnight until dawn in the Gay 90s lounge in The Last Frontier Hotel?

A. The Mary Kaye Trio.

━━━ ❧ ━━━

Q. Who were the members of the Mary Kaye Trio?

A. Brother and sister Norman and Mary Kaye, and Frankie Ross.

━━━ ❧ ━━━

Q. What "fabulous" hotel/casino on the Las Vegas Strip opened the day after Christmas 1946?

A. The Flamingo.

Q. Who was the star at the Flamingo's grand opening?

A. The "Schnoz," Jimmy Durante.

Q. What did Flamingo builder "Bugsy" Siegel do to ensure a grand opening attendance of notables?

A. At his expense, he had several planes bring Hollywood stars and other celebrities from Los Angeles.

Q. Durante and his pal, Eddie Jackson, did what unusual "act" while on stage?

A. They demolished a $1,600 piano.

Q. Pearl Bailey, Ted Lewis, the Mills Brothers, Dean Martin, Jerry Lewis, Bo Jangles, and Spike Jones and his band were early performers at what Las Vegas Strip hotel?

A. The Flamingo.

Q. At what two casinos in Glitter Gulch were huge neon marquees erected in 1946?

A. The Golden Nugget and the Eldorado Club.

Q. What are three commonly used nicknames for Las Vegas?

A. Glitter Gulch (Fremont St.), Sin City, and Lost Wages.

Q. What was one of the greatest publicity stunts for Las Vegas in the late 1940s?

A. A tall, neon, cowboy sign named Vegas Vic stood tall over Glitter Gulch, greeting visitors with a drawled "Howdy, Podner" and a wave of his arm.

———— ∞∞ ————

Q. What were two highly popular radio shows broadcast from Las Vegas?

A. Lum and Abner and Amos and Andy.

———— ∞∞ ————

Q. What was the location of Lum and Abner's "Jot 'em down store"?

A. The Little Church of the West.

———— ∞∞ ————

Q. From what hotel did the Amos and Andy show broadcast?

A. The Flamingo.

———— ∞∞ ————

Q. What singer made his debut at the El Rancho Vegas?

A. Frankie Laine.

———— ∞∞ ————

Q. Who was one of the first Hollywood stars to make the transition from films to on-stage performances in Las Vegas?

A. Dorothy Dandridge, at the Club Bingo.

———— ∞∞ ————

Q. Dorothy achieved what "first" in Hollywood?

A. She was the first black entertainer to achieve star status.

Q. What was the name of the organization formed in the 1940s to promote Las Vegas?

A. The Desert Sea News Bureau.

Q. The Thunderbird's "world's largest marquee" cost how much?

A. A quarter of a million dollars.

Q. How many lights were in the marquee?

A. 37,000.

Q. How much neon tubing was in the Thunderbird's marquee?

A. Eight miles.

Q. How tall were the marquee's letters, which spelled out "Thunderbird"?

A. Six feet.

Q. Who were some of the star entertainers in the Navajo main show room?

A. Harry Belafonte, Patty Paige, Burl Ives, and "Lonesome" George Gobel.

Q. What were some of the musicals from Broadway shows at the Thunderbird?

A. "Flower Drum Song," "South Pacific," "Paint Your Wagon," and "Guys and Dolls."

Q. How many rooms did the Desert Inn have and what did it cost to build it?

A. It had 300 rooms and cost $1.5 million to build.

———⊗⊗⊗———

Q. Who starred at the grand opening of the Desert Inn?

A. Edgar Bergan with Charlie McCarthy and Mortimer Snerd.

———⊗⊗⊗———

Q. What dance group and what orchestra leader played at the grand opening?

A. The Don Arden Dancers and the Ray Noble Orchestra.

———⊗⊗⊗———

Q. Who was the singer with six gold records who made his Las Vegas debut in the lounge at the Desert Inn?

A. Billy Eckstine.

———⊗⊗⊗———

Q. Who made his debut at the Desert Inn showroom in 1951?

A. Frank Sinatra.

———⊗⊗⊗———

Q. What zany entertainer won over $38,000 at a craps table at the Desert Inn?

A. Harpo Marx.

———⊗⊗⊗———

Q. What type of shows were featured at the old Silver Slipper?

A. Burlesque.

Q. What sign identified the Silver Slipper?

A. A huge lady's slipper with hundreds of lights.

Q. Who was the star in the Silver Slipper showroom for many years?

A. Hank Henry.

Q. Who bought the downtown Las Vegas Eldorado Club in 1951?

A. Benny Binion.

Q. What new name did Binion give the Eldorado?

A. The Horseshoe Club.

Q. Binion also set up a high stakes poker game between what gamblers?

A. Johnny Moss and Nick the Greek.

Q. The high stakes poker game became a marathon that lasted how long?

A. Five months.

Q. How much did Moss win?

A. An estimated $2 million, according to some reports.

Q. What resulted from all the attention given this poker game?

A. The World Series of Poker was established.

———— ⊗⊗⊙ ————

Q. What price did Binion later pay for Del Webb's next-door Mint Hotel?

A. $27 million.

———— ⊗⊗⊙ ————

Q. Combining the Mint and the Horseshoe did what?

A. It doubled the size of the casino and added a 24-story tower hotel with 296 rooms.

———— ⊗⊗⊙ ————

Q. Who bought the old Bingo Club on the Las Vegas Strip?

A. Milton Prell.

———— ⊗⊗⊙ ————

Q. What did Prell build on the old Bingo Club property?

A. The Sahara Hotel/Casino, known as the Jewel of the Desert.

———— ⊗⊗⊙ ————

Q. What greeted visitors to the Sahara?

A. Camel caravan statues and doormen dressed like sheiks.

———— ⊗⊗⊙ ————

Q. Who were among the first entertainers in the Sahara's Casbah Lounge?

A. Belle Barth, Don Rickles, the Platters, Rusty Warren and her "Knockers Up" show, and Louie Prima and Keely Smith, to name a few.

Q. Stan Erwin, of the Sahara Hotel, brought what famous English singing group to Las Vegas for their only appearance here?

A. The Beatles.

Q. Scheduled to play in the Sahara, the turnout for the Beatles was so large the show had to be moved to what other site?

A. The Las Vegas Convention Center.

Q. What was an earlier name of the Sands Hotel?

A. The LaRue Restaurant.

Q. When the old LaRue Restaurant was sold and the new owners decided to remodel the place and give it a new name, why did they choose the Sands?

A. Because of all the sand they got in their shoes as they walked around the construction site.

Q. Who were some of the first big stars to play in the Sands' Copa Room?

A. Frank Sinatra, Jack Benny, Wayne Newton, Red Skelton, Rita Hayworth, Talulah Bankhead, Dean Martin and Jerry Lewis, George Burns, and Debbie Reynolds.

Q. What hotel was the first to sign top entertainers to exclusive contracts?

A. The Sands.

Q. The Sands got international publicity when it did what to keep the crap shooters cool in the heat of the summer?

A. They put a floating crap table in the swimming pool.

Q. What was the first name of the replica of a Mississippi riverboat constructed in 1954 on the Boulder Highway?

A. The Desert Showboat Motor Hotel, which later became the Showboat Hotel and Casino.

Q. How much did it cost to build the original Showboat?

A. $2 million.

Q. What was the first Las Vegas resort to host international bowling tournaments?

A. The Showboat.

Q. With construction of many other hotel/casinos on the Boulder Highway in later years, this road became known locally as what?

A. The Boulder Strip, or "the second strip."

Q. The Showboat became very popular for country-western music. Who were some of the top stars to play there?

A. Tex Ritter, Red Foley, Homer and Jethro, Roy Acuff, and Hank Thompson.

Q. Who were some of the top lounge acts on the Strip in the 1950s and 1960s?

A. The Mary Kaye Trio, Benny Goodman, Don Rickles, Redd Foxx, Checkmates, Rip Taylor, Peggy Lee, and Sarah Vaughan.

Q. What was the 1989 community event in Mesquite that was patterned after a major attraction in Spain and was a "first" for a Nevada town?

A. The Running of the Bulls.

Q. Marathon runners come to Las Vegas for what event?

A. The Las Vegas International Marathon.

Q. What is the name and location of a major event for photographers?

A. The Shooting the West Photography Workshop in Winnemucca.

Q. The annual Snowfest is held where?

A. North Lake Tahoe and Truckee.

Q. Along with Elko, what other Nevada town hosts a gathering of cowboy poets?

A. Carson City, with its annual Cowboy Poetry and Jubilee.

Q. The works and traditions of Native Americans are a celebration theme where?

A. At the Native American Arts Festival in Henderson.

Q. Year-round water sports attractions of all kinds are right outside the doors of major hotels/casinos in what Nevada town?

A. Laughlin, on the Colorado River.

Q. An important part of Nevada's history is relived at what celebration?

A. Henderson's Heritage Days.

Q. Bikers from all over ride into what town for what big celebration?

A. The Harley River Run in Laughlin.

Q. Art exhibits are the feature of what annual event in what Nevada town?

A. The Clark County Art Show, held in Boulder City.

Q. Music lovers flock to what Nevada city for a celebration?

A. Reno, for the annual Reno Jazz Festival.

Q. What city hosts the annual PGA Senior Classic golf tournament?

A. Las Vegas.

Q. What Nevada town hosts the Grand Prix Motorcycle Race?

A. Virginia City.

———⧳———

Q. What town on the Extraterrestrial Highway has its special day?

A. Rachael has its Rachael Day annual celebration.

———⧳———

Q. The Silver State Classic Challenge Auto Race is held where?

A. Ely.

———⧳———

Q. Armed Forces Day is a three-day event in what Nevada town?

A. Hawthorne.

———⧳———

Q. May is a big month for the town of Mesquite, with what two celebrations?

A. Cinco de Mayo and Mesquite Days.

———⧳———

Q. The Cinco de Mayo Run/Walk is held in what Nevada town?

A. Sparks.

———⧳———

Q. Water sports are the main attraction at what celebration?

A. Laughlin River Days.

Q. Reno hosts what special event for table tennis players?

A. The Far West Regional Wheelchair Tennis Championship.

———∞∞∞———

Q. Rodeos are highly popular throughout Nevada. What is the name of the annual event in Fallon?

A. The Silver State International Rodeo.

———∞∞∞———

Q. What Nevada city hosts the annual National Basque Festival?

A. Elko.

———∞∞∞———

Q. The city of Mesquite observes the Fourth of July with what two-day celebration?

A. The Independence Day Water Festival.

———∞∞∞———

Q. The Old West is alive and well at what celebration in Fallon?

A. The All-Indian Rodeo, Stampede, and Pioneer Days.

———∞∞∞———

Q. Where is the Way It Was Rodeo held?

A. Virginia City.

———∞∞∞———

Q. The "Bard" is remembered at what August fête in Incline Village?

A. Shakespeare at Sand Harbor.

Q. Where is the Land Speed Opener held?

A. At the Bonneville Salt Flats, Wendover.

Q. What city is the home of the Nevada State Fair each August?

A. Reno.

Q. The National Championship Air Races are held where?

A. In Reno (Stead Airport).

Q. A special class of auto enthusiasts converge on Virginia City for what event?

A. The Ferrari Hill Climb.

Q. Of the 13 largest hotels in the world, how many are in Nevada?

A. Twelve.

Q. By whom, when, and in what Nevada town was the popular carnival ride, the Ferris wheel, invented?

A. George Ferris invented the ride in Carson City in 1893.

Q. What city and its landmark are the sites of John Wayne's last movie, "The Shootist"?

A. The Robinson Krebs-Peterson House in Carson City.

Q. Who is the female country-western singer who became an overnight sensation while still in her teens?

A. Tanya Tucker.

———∞∞∞———

Q. In what Nevada town did Tanya live when she became a star?

A. Henderson.

———∞∞∞———

Q. What was the title of the hit single that gave her instant stardom?

A. "Delta Dawn."

———∞∞∞———

Q. As a teenage singing star, who was Tanya's idol?

A. Elvis Presley.

———∞∞∞———

Q. What is one of the most popular tourist attractions at Binion's Horseshoe Club in downtown Las Vegas?

A. You can have your picture taken standing alongside a display case containing $1 million.

———∞∞∞———

Q. What central Nevada town hosts three annual festivals, and what are they?

A. Austin is the site of Gridley Days, the Claim Jumpers Bike Festival, and a Rock and Bottle Show.

———∞∞∞———

Q. Where is the Native American Snow Dance held?

A. Incline Village.

Q. An annual bluegrass festival is held in what southern Nevada town?

A. Logandale.

Q. When in 1999 will Nevada's 15th Month Millennium Celebration begin?

A. October 31.

Q. Mesquite's Christmas celebration is known by what name?

A. The Tannenbaum Christmas Festival.

Q. Where is Christmas in the Nighttime Skies held?

A. Elko.

Q. Las Vegas goes western for what major event each December?

A. The National Finals Rodeo.

Q. What city hosts the annual Buck 'n Ball?

A. Reno.

Q. What is one of the most decorative holiday events in southern Nevada?

A. The annual Parade of Lights on Lake Mead.

Q. What was the major factor that resulted in Las Vegas far outdistancing Reno as a gambling entertainment center in the mid-1900s?

A. Reno severely restricted gaming development while Las Vegas went full speed ahead, albeit the development of major resorts on the Strip are not in Las Vegas but in unincorporated areas of Clark County.

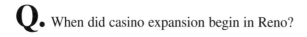

Q. When did casino expansion begin in Reno?

A. In 1972, following repeal of its "red line" restrictions on gambling.

Q. In 1954, who bought the 101 Club in North Las Vegas?

A. Don Laughlin, founder of the Colorado River resort town that bears his name.

Q. What was Laughlin's first purchase on the Colorado River?

A. A bankrupt, boarded-up, eight-room motel on six acres of riverfront property.

Q. How many hotel/casinos are there in Laughlin?

A. Eleven.

Q. How long is the Desperado roller coaster at Buffalo Bill's in Primm?

A. More than a mile (5,483 feet).

Q. What length of time does a ride on the Desperado last?

A. Two minutes and 43 seconds.

———∞∞∞———

Q. How high is the roller coaster's second drop?

A. 155 feet.

———∞∞∞———

Q. The Desperado roller coaster reaches near-zero gravity how many times?

A. Three.

———∞∞∞———

Q. What is the only town in Nevada that prohibits gambling?

A. Boulder City, in Clark County.

———∞∞∞———

Q. At what Las Vegas hotel did Cab Calloway star?

A. The old Royal Nevada, now part of the Stardust Hotel/Casino.

———∞∞∞———

Q. What was the first skyscraper hotel/casino on the Las Vegas Strip?

A. The Riviera, at nine stories.

———∞∞∞———

Q. When did the Last Frontier Hotel change its name to the New Frontier Hotel?

A. 1956.

Q. Who was one of the first singers to appear in the New Frontier lounge?

A. Elvis Presley, in 1956.

Q. The first television station in Las Vegas began broadcasting where?

A. KSHO-TV operated from a one-room office in the Fremont Hotel.

Q. What Las Vegas hotel initiated "champagne flights" for its guests?

A. The one-time Hacienda Motor Hotel, at the far south end of the Strip.

Q. Where was the first lighted golf course in Las Vegas?

A. At the old Hacienda Hotel.

Q. What was the first interracial hotel in Las Vegas?

A. The Moulin Rouge.

Q. Who was a host/greeter when the Moulin Rouge opened in the mid-1950s?

A. Boxer Joe Louis.

Q. The Moulin Rouge declared bankruptcy how long after the hotel opened?

A. Six months.

Q. The Moulin Rouge is listed in what historical record?

A. The National Register of Historic Places.

———∞———

Q. What was at the entrance of the Dunes Hotel/Casino when it first opened?

A. A 30-foot-tall statue of an Arabian Sultan named Mr. Sinbad.

———∞———

Q. By what year had the Dunes failed financially?

A. 1956.

———∞———

Q. Under new ownership, who was the man who made the Dunes a leading hotel/casino?

A. Major Riddle.

———∞———

Q. When did the Dunes build its new 24-story high-rise, featuring dining and dancing on the top floor?

A. In the early 1960s.

———∞———

Q. How tall was the famous Dunes marquee, and what was its cost?

A. The largest free-standing marquee in the world was 185 feet tall, built at a cost of $318,000.

———∞———

Q. What was one of the longest-running shows ever on the Las Vegas Strip?

A. Casino de Paris, at the Dunes.

Q. What Las Vegas Strip hotel was called the Tiffany of the Strip?

A. The Tropicana.

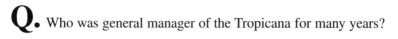

Q. Who was general manager of the Tropicana for many years?

A. Bob Cannon.

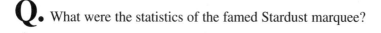

Q. Who was the owner of a gambling ship off the California coast who came to Las Vegas in the mid-1950s and built the Stardust Hotel/Casino?

A. Anthony Stralla (better known as Tony Carnaro).

Q. What were the statistics of the famed Stardust marquee?

A. It was 216 feet long, 27 feet high, with 32,000 feet of wiring, 7,100 feet of neon lighting, and 11,000 multicolored light bulbs.

Q. What was the name of the long-standing show at the Stardust?

A. The Lido de Paris.

Q. What were the room rates at the Stardust when it opened?

A. $6 a night.

Q. What was the name of the largest-ever resort without a casino built on the Las Vegas Strip?

A. The Tally Ho, which opened in February 1963.

Q. How long did the Tally Ho continue to operate?

A. About six months. (Later it became the Aladdin, with full gambling.)

———∞∞∞———

Q. In what year did the late billionaire Howard Hughes and his entourage come to Las Vegas?

A. 1966.

———∞∞∞———

Q. What entertainer holds the record for the greatest number of performances on the Las Vegas Strip?

A. Wayne Newton.

———∞∞∞———

Q. What was the first national organization of public officials ever to hold its annual convention in Las Vegas?

A. The 1966 National League of Cities convention.

———∞∞∞———

Q. What Las Vegas Strip hotel served as headquarters for this record-breaking convention?

A. Caesars Palace.

———∞∞∞———

Q. What was the first "family gambling casino" built on the Las Vegas Strip?

A. Circus Circus.

Q. In what way did Circus Circus actually cater to families?

A. With many games and other attractions for kids, including actual aerial circus acts over the casino area.

Q. What was the size of what was claimed to be the largest casino in the world at the Union Plaza?

A. One and one-half acres.

Q. How tall was the old Landmark Hotel/Casino?

A. Thirty-one stories, including a 3-story dome at the top, making it the tallest building in Nevada.

Q. When was the grand opening of the International?

A. July 2, 1969.

Q. Who was the showroom headliner at the grand opening of the International, and what was she paid?

A. Barbra Streisand, who was paid $100,000 a week.

Q. Who was the next singer to star at the International?

A. Elvis Presley.

Q. The International became the Hilton when it was purchased for what price?

A. $45 million.

Q. When did the MGM Grand Hotel/Casino (now Bally's) open on the Las Vegas Strip?

A. December 5, 1973.

Q. Then the world's largest hotel, how many rooms did the MGM Grand have?

A. 2,100 rooms and suites, built at a cost of $120 million.

Q. Who costarred for the MGM Grand Opening?

A. Dean Martin and Barbara Eden.

Q. In his many years of show business, what famous band leader made his first Las Vegas appearance at the MGM Grand?

A. Lawrence Welk and his Champagne Music.

Q. Billionaire Kirk Kerkorian built what Las Vegas hotels?

A. The International and the MGM Grand.

Q. Jay Sarno built what two major hotels on the Las Vegas Strip?

A. Caesars Palace and Circus Circus.

HISTORY

Q. When was the first seal of the Territory of Nevada adopted?

A. 1861.

Q. The official Nevada state seal was adopted in what year?

A. 1866.

Q. What was the Nevada Territory's motto, adopted in 1861?

A. "Volens et Potens," meaning "Willing and Able."

Q. What motto is incorporated in the seal adopted in 1866?

A. "All for Our Country."

Q. In what year was Nevada's first official state flag authorized?

A. 1905.

Q. How many stars appeared on Nevada's first flag?

A. Thirty-six. Nevada was the 36th state admitted to the Union.

Q. Only one flag with this first design still exists. It was later bought by the Nevada National Guard for what price?

A. $30.65.

———⊶⊷———

Q. In what year did the Nevada legislature repeal the Flag Act of 1905 and create the second design for the flag?

A. 1915.

———⊶⊷———

Q. When was the third official flag of Nevada created by the legislature?

A. In 1929, from a design chosen in 1927.

———⊶⊷———

Q. There was a significant omission in the design of the third flag. What was it?

A. Nowhere in the flag did the word "Nevada" appear.

———⊶⊷———

Q. How many of these flags existed, even seven years after its adoption?

A. Fewer than six. Even the USS *Nevada* still carried the 1915 flag.

———⊶⊷———

Q. Due to an error in previous legislation, what action did the 1991 legislature take regarding the flag?

A. This action placed the word "Nevada" in a different location in the flag.

Q. What color is the body of the Nevada state flag?

A. Cobalt blue.

———— ∞∞∞ ————

Q. The Nevada state flag adopted in 1915 contained what significant error?

A. It had 37 stars instead of 36 (Nevada was the 36th state).

———— ∞∞∞ ————

Q. What is the title of Nevada's official state song?

A. "Home Means Nevada."

———— ∞∞∞ ————

Q. Who wrote the song, and in what year did the legislature adopt it?

A. Mrs. Bertha Raffetto of Reno. Her song was made official in 1933.

———— ∞∞∞ ————

Q. By what procedure are official features, emblems, and so on, of the state adopted?

A. An official act of the legislature is required.

———— ∞∞∞ ————

Q. What animal was designated in what year as the state's official animal?

A. The desert bighorn sheep, in 1973.

———— ∞∞∞ ————

Q. What are Nevada's official colors, and when were they designated?

A. Silver and blue, in 1983.

Q. What is Nevada's official state fish, and when was it adopted?

A. The Lahontan cutthroat trout, in 1981.

Q. What is the official state flower, and in what year was it adopted?

A. Sagebrush, in 1959.

Q. Nevada has two official state trees. What are they, and when were they so designated?

A. The single-leaf pinion in 1953, and the bristlecone pine in 1987.

Q. The official metal of Nevada, silver, was chosen when?

A. 1977.

Q. What is Nevada's state reptile, and when was it adopted?

A. The desert tortoise, in 1989.

Q. Nevada's official fossil is also the name of a state park. What is the name, and in what year was it designated?

A. *Ichthyosaur*, in 1977.

Q. In what year did the legislature first declare that all state government offices would be closed on October 31, Nevada's Admission Day state holiday?

A. 1931.

Q. When was Nevada's capitol in Carson City built?

A. 1870–71.

───── ∞ ─────

Q. Who were Nevada's first two U.S. Senators?

A. James W. Nye and William M. Stewart, both Republicans.

───── ∞ ─────

Q. Who was Nevada's first representative in Congress?

A. Henry G. Worthington, a Republican.

───── ∞ ─────

Q. On what date was the city of Las Vegas founded?

A. May 15, 1905.

───── ∞ ─────

Q. What was the "kick-off" event that founded Las Vegas?

A. Officials of the San Pedro, Los Angeles, and Salt Lake Railroad Company conducted an auction of townsites, with more than 1,000 people present.

───── ∞ ─────

Q. Why was the Las Vegas site chosen for development?

A. It is located about midway between Los Angeles and Salt Lake City, and water was abundant from the many springs and artesian wells.

───── ∞ ─────

Q. When did the Mormons come into the Las Vegas Valley where they established a mission, built a fort, and engaged in mining and agriculture?

A. 1855.

Q. Why are the years 1831 and 1832 notable in Nevada's history?

A. This marked the beginning of annual Mexican trading caravans, which passed through the Las Vegas Valley en route from Santa Fe to Los Angeles.

Q. Where did Las Vegas get its name?

A. Its name has a Spanish origin, "Las Vegas" meaning "The Meadows."

Q. What Nevada city has an Indian reservation wholly within its city limits?

A. A Paiute reservation is in the city of Las Vegas.

Q. The Spanish Trail, which ran from Santa Fe to Los Angeles, passing through the Las Vegas Valley, was used during what years by early settlers?

A. From 1830 until 1848.

Q. Who was the first mayor of Las Vegas?

A. Peter Buol, who served from 1911 to 1913.

Q. How many people have served as mayor of Las Vegas from 1911 through 1998?

A. Fifteen.

Q. Las Vegas' first city hall was originally built and known as what?

A. The War Memorial Building.

Q. Who built the first major commercial structure in Tonopah?

A. Frank Golden, a Reno jeweler and entrepreneur.

Q. Who was Tasker Oddie?

A. An early attorney from Belmont, and Nevada's governor from 1911 to 1915.

Q. Tonopah's first ore was smelted where?

A. It was hauled by horse and wagon to Austin, then by rail to Salt Lake City.

Q. How many tons of silver and gold ore have been produced from Tonopah area mines?

A. In excess of five million tons.

Q. At today's market prices, what would be the value of precious metals mined from the Tonopah district?

A. In excess of $1,200,000,000.

Q. What is the largest city in Nevada that doesn't have a chief of police?

A. Las Vegas. The city police department and the Clark County Sheriff's Office consolidated in the early 1970s, and what is now the Las Vegas Metropolitan Police Department is headed by an elected county sheriff.

Q. What is the most famous building in Goldfield?

A. The historic Goldfield Hotel, once considered the most luxurious inn between Salt Lake City and San Francisco.

Q. What was Nevada's largest town during the gold strike era?

A. Goldfield.

Q. What are the three nicknames for the state of Nevada?

A. The Silver State, Battle Born, and the Sagebrush State.

Q. What is Nevada's official precious gemstone, and when was it adopted?

A. Virgin Valley black fire opal, adopted in 1987.

Q. What is Nevada's official semiprecious gemstone, and when was it adopted?

A. Nevada turquoise, adopted in 1987.

Q. When did Nevada grant women the right to vote in state and local elections?

A. 1914.

———∞∞∞———

Q. In what year did legislation limit the governor to two four-year terms?

A. 1970.

———∞∞∞———

Q. When was the constitution amended to prohibit a state personal income tax?

A. In the general elections in 1988 and 1990.

———∞∞∞———

Q. When did the Nevada Legislature approve the Sales and Use Tax Act?

A. 1955.

———∞∞∞———

Q. What was the major provision of this legislation?

A. It established the state's first sales tax, at a rate of 2 percent.

———∞∞∞———

Q. Since the sales tax was established, the legislature has increased this tax how many times?

A. Twice, by adding 2.25 percent in 1967 and the same amount in 1969.

Q. For what purposes were these sales tax increases approved?

A. For support of schools in 1967, and in 1969 for support of cities and counties.

Q. In the 1998 general election, voters in Clark County approved an additional 0.25 percent sales tax for what purpose?

A. To help pay construction costs to bring more water into the Las Vegas Valley.

Q. What major change in election laws was approved by the 1975 legislature?

A. The bill gives the voters the option of voting in primary and general elections for "none of these candidates" for all state elective offices.

Q. What happens if "none of these candidates" gets the most votes?

A. The actual candidate receiving the most votes wins.

Q. Has "none of these candidates" ever finished first in a Nevada election?

A. Yes, in the 1976 and 1986 primary elections.

Q. How many Nevada counties approved by vote the constitutional amendment that gave women the right to vote?

A. It was approved in 12 of the 16 counties.

Q. Who was the first female to run for a federal office from Nevada?

A. Anne Martin, who ran (and lost) as an Independent candidate for U.S. Senator in 1918 and 1920.

———∞∞———

Q. It was 60 years before another woman ran for the U.S. Senate. Who was she?

A. Mary Gojack was the Democratic nominee in 1980, but lost the election.

———∞∞———

Q. What major change in Nevada politics resulted from the 1980 official U.S. Census?

A. A second Congressional District was created, giving Nevada two members in the U.S. House of Representatives.

———∞∞———

Q. What was unique about the 1982 election for the first Representative from District 2?

A. There were four candidates, all women.

———∞∞———

Q. How many Nevada women have served as U.S. Senators?

A. None.

———∞∞———

Q. Who was the first Nevada woman to serve in the United States Congress?

A. Barbara Vucanovich, who won the 1982 election and was re-elected at each subsequent election until her retirement in 1996.

Q. How many Nevada women have ever been elected to Congress?

A. Two. Barbara Vucanovich and Shelley Berkley, a Democrat, who won the District 1 race in November 1998.

Q. Who was Nevada's longest-serving representative in Congress?

A. Walter Baring, who served ten nonsuccessive terms.

Q. What are the six statewide, or "constitutional," elective offices in Nevada?

A. Governor, Lt. Governor, Attorney General, Secretary of State, Treasurer, and Controller.

Q. How many of the six constitutional offices have women won?

A. Four.

Q. What was the first constitutional seat to be won by a woman?

A. Republican Patty D. Cafferata was elected state treasurer in 1982.

Q. Who was the first woman to win the primary election and appear on the general election ballot for governor?

A. Republican Shirley Crumpler, in 1974.

Q. Who was the first woman on a general election ballot for Treasurer?

A. Clara Cunningham, a Republican, who ran for the office in 1926.

Q. Who was the first woman to be elected Lt. Governor?

A. Republican Sue Wagner, elected in 1990.

Q. Who was the first woman elected to the Nevada legislature?

A. Republican Sadie D. Hurst, elected to the Assembly in 1918.

Q. Who was the first woman attorney to serve in the Assembly?

A. Ruth Averill, a Republican from Nye County, elected in 1921.

Q. Who was the first woman attorney to be elected to the State Senate?

A. Lori Lipman Brown, a Democrat from Clark County, elected in 1992.

Q. Who was the first woman to be elected as District Court Judge in Nevada?

A. Miriam Shearing in Clark County, in 1983.

Q. Who was the first woman to be elected to the Nevada Supreme Court?

A. Miriam Shearing, in 1992.

Q. Who was the first woman to hold elective office in Clark County?

A. Mary E. McCarthy, a Republican, who was assessor in 1917.

Q. Who is the only Nevada governor ever to serve more than two terms?

A. Democrat Bob Miller, who served as acting governor from January 3, 1989 to January 7, 1991, and was elected to two consecutive terms, serving through 1998.

Q. What are the two county seats that have remained since the establishment of the Nevada Territory?

A. Carson City, Carson City County, and Virginia City, Storey County.

Q. How many cities or towns in Nevada have served as county seats since 1861?

A. Thirty-two.

Q. In all Nevada's history, what was the lengthiest battle over the location of the county seat?

A. The fight between the towns of Austin and Battle Mountain to serve as the county seat of Lander County lasted more than 50 years.

Q. Which town eventually won the county seat war?

A. In 1979, the Lander County seat was moved from Austin to Battle Mountain.

Q. County seats in Nevada may be changed by legislative action or by special county elections. How many times did the legislature change county seats?

A. Thirteen.

⸺⸙⸺

Q. When was Nevada's most populous county created, and from what?

A. Clark County (Las Vegas) was created out of Lincoln County in 1909.

⸺⸙⸺

Q. When did the legislature create the last county in Nevada?

A. Bullfrog County was created out of a portion of Nye County in 1987, and two years later, in 1989, it was abolished and the original boundaries of Nye County restored.

⸺⸙⸺

Q. What is now Lincoln County was first traversed by European explorers in what years?

A. 1549 to 1775, when the Spaniards first explored this region of the southwest.

⸺⸙⸺

Q. Many of the first individual and family settlers of the town of Alamo came from where?

A. Fredonia, Arizona.

⸺⸙⸺

Q. When was the Alamo post office established?

A. May 12, 1905.

Q. When was gold discovered in the Pahranagat Valley?

A. 1890 and 1891.

Q. Who founded the town of Delamar?

A. Capt. John DeLamar of Montana, who purchased major mining claims in 1893.

Q. Delamar gold production exceeded all other mines in Nevada until what year?

A. 1909.

Q. When did gold production stop in Delamar?

A. The operation was closed in 1909, and reopened briefly from 1929 to 1934.

Q. By what name was the town of Caliente first known?

A. Dutch Flat.

Q. Where are Robbers Roost and Grapevine Canyon?

A. About 13 miles south of the town of Caliente, on S.R. 317.

Q. What link do they have to Nevada's early history?

A. They served as hideouts or escape routes for outlaw bands, including Butch Cassidy and the Sundance Kid. Routes out of the canyon are by foot or horseback.

Q. Where did the town of Pioche get its name?

A. It was named after Francois L. S. Pioche, a San Francisco financier.

———∞———

Q. Where did the town of Panaca get its name?

A. "Pa-na-ka" is a southern Paiute word meaning "metal."

———∞———

Q. What was the name of a historic mining camp about ten miles south of Pioche?

A. It was first named Camp Ely, but later became Bullionville.

———∞———

Q. What event touched off the 1899 copper boom in the Ely area?

A. The discovery by Dan McDonald of the Ruth mine, which he named after his three-year-old daughter.

———∞———

Q. How long was the Nevada Northern Railway line, built in 1905–1906 to haul ore from copper mines in the Ely area?

A. 150 miles.

———∞———

Q. What was the fate of the original Old Ruth mining town?

A. Much of it is buried beneath the huge piles of tailings.

———∞———

Q. The mining town of New Ruth resulted from what event?

A. In the 1950s the Kennecott Copper Corporation's company-owned buildings and houses were moved a short distance when mining operations were expanded.

Q. What was the size of the Liberty Pit, the largest mining pit in Nevada, when it was abandoned by Kennecott in 1967?

A. Over a mile long, over a half-mile wide, and nearly 1,000 feet deep.

Q. What was the value of the copper, gold, and silver produced during the first half of the twentieth century from mines in the Copper Country triangle near Ely?

A. Nearly a billion dollars.

Q. What mining camp in the Ely area was noted for its sinful reputation?

A. Reipetown, founded in 1907, five miles northwest of Ely, had 16 saloons providing liquor, gambling, and prostitution.

Q. By what name is the area where the settlements of Copper Flat, Kimberly, Ruth, Reipetown, and Veteran were located known as?

A. Copper Flat.

Q. What action was taken in 1970 to assure preservation of the old Mormon fort in Las Vegas?

A. The property was acquired by the city of Las Vegas. It is now the Old Las Vegas Mormon Fort State Historic Park.

Q. In what year did Congress establish a mail route from Salt Lake City to San Diego, by way of Las Vegas?

A. 1854.

Q. What was the first town in Clark County to have an airport?

A. Boulder City, where TWA established service soon after the Hoover Dam was built.

———∞———

Q. Schellbourne, in the foothills of the Schell Creek mountain range in northern Nevada, was home to what other people long before it became a mining camp?

A. The Shoshone Indians.

———∞———

Q. The silver mining boom in the town of Ward lasted how long?

A. From 1872 to 1882.

———∞———

Q. During the gold rush to Virginia City in 1859–1860, in what Nevada town did the army station troops to protect the gold seekers headed west?

A. Schellbourne.

———∞———

Q. Where and in what year was Nevada's first chamber of commerce established?

A. In the town of Elko in 1907.

———∞———

Q. Why was the town of Elko founded?

A. As a railroad-promoted townsite and railhead for the White Pine County mines.

Q. The difficulty of the Humboldt route led to the opening of a more southerly route through what area?

A. The area is known as Ruby Valley.

Q. Elko was "given birth" the last week of December 1868 by what event?

A. The Central Pacific Railroad arrived on its push eastward.

Q. In January 1869, Elko was still a "tent city," but during that month building lots began selling for what price?

A. $300 to $500 each.

Q. When was Elko County created and the town of Elko made the county seat?

A. March 5, 1869.

Q. In area, how does Elko County rank with other counties in the United States?

A. It is the sixth largest, with 17,181 square miles.

Q. In what month did the Central Pacific and Union Pacific Railroads meet?

A. May 1869.

Q. Who was the first and only woman to be legally hanged in Nevada?

A. Elizabeth Potts and her husband Josiah were hanged in 1890 in the Elko jailyard for committing murder.

Q. European immigrants from what area played an important role in Elko's early history?

A. Basque men from the Pyrenees Mountains between Spain and France were employed on sheep ranches throughout the American West.

Q. What Nevada town in 1926 became the terminus for the nation's first commercial airmail flight?

A. Elko.

Q. Who served as the first president of the Elko Chamber of Commerce?

A. W. I. Smith, who took office April 22, 1907.

Q. What mining town in Nevada in the 1870s had the dubious distinction of being the "roughest, toughest, and wildest gun-toting town" in the West?

A. Pioche.

Q. What event was the beginning of ore strikes in the Pioche area?

A. Indians from the Santa Clara Paiute tribe offered to show William Hamblin an outcropping of ore in exchange for food and clothing.

Q. Mineral production in Lincoln County during the 1870s was second only to what other area in Nevada?

A. The Comstock in the Virginia City area.

Q. What was the date and cause of a disastrous fire in Pioche?

A. On September 15, 1871, a restaurant caught fire during a celebration of Mexican Independence. The town was virtually destroyed, and 13 men were killed.

Q. Who was the first woman in the nation to found a national bank?

A. Edna Howard Covert Plummer founded the Farmer's and Merchant's Bank in Eureka in July 1920.

Q. This Nevada pioneer is credited with what other national "first"?

A. She was the first female district attorney in the nation and served in Eureka County in 1918.

Q. How many cemeteries are located in the Eureka area?

A. Five.

Q. The site of Eureka's cemeteries has been known by what names?

A. Graveyard Flat, or as known in the 1880s, Death Valley.

Q. How many smelters were in operation in the Eureka district at one time?

A. Sixteen.

———❧———

Q. Smoke from these smelters was often so heavy that Eureka became known as what?

A. The Pittsburgh of the West.

———❧———

Q. What is the history of Eureka's Tannehill log cabin?

A. It is believed to have been the first house built in Eureka, around 1865.

———❧———

Q. What was the name of Eureka's first permanent church, and when was it built?

A. Saint James Episcopal Church, built in 1872.

———❧———

Q. In what building were the first movies shown in Eureka?

A. In the Opera House, which became the Eureka Theater.

———❧———

Q. During what period did a U.S. Mint operate in Carson City?

A. 1870–1893.

———❧———

Q. What state facility is now housed in the old Mint building?

A. The Nevada State Museum.

Q. What historic event brought an end to the Pony Express?

A. Completion of the first transcontinental railroad.

———❧———

Q. What was the first federal reclamation project in the United States?

A. The Newlands Project in western Nevada.

———❧———

Q. What was a major construction feature of the Newlands Project?

A. The construction of Lahontan Dam in Churchill County.

———❧———

Q. In what year was the Newlands Project completed?

A. 1914.

———❧———

Q. The era of Eureka's silver boom spanned what years?

A. 1870–1890.

———❧———

Q. What central Nevada mining town had its own Chinatown?

A. Eureka.

———❧———

Q. How many major fires did Eureka have between 1876 and 1880?

A. Four.

———❧———

Q. When did the Pony Express run through Nevada?

A. From April 1860 to October 1861.

Q. Between what east and west cities did the Pony Express carry mail?

A. St. Joseph, MO, and Sacramento, CA.

Q. What was the total length of the Pony Express route?

A. About 2,000 miles.

Q. How long did it take riders to make a one-way trip?

A. About ten days.

Q. Pony Express riders averaged how many miles per trip?

A. About 33.

Q. How many times did they change horses during their ride?

A. Twice, about every 10 to 15 miles.

Q. In what year did the Virginia and Truckee Railroad (V&T) link Reno and Virginia City?

A. 1872.

Q. Where did Reno get its name?

A. It was named after Gen. Jesse Lee Reno, a Union officer in the Civil War.

Q. In Nevada's history, how many election recounts have been made for statewide offices?

A. Five.

———∞∞∞———

Q. How many of these recounts resulted in a reversal of election results?

A. None.

———∞∞∞———

Q. What action made Nevada's U.S. Senator Harry Reid the highest-ranking senator in Nevada's history?

A. On December 2, 1998, he was elected democratic whip in Congress.

———∞∞∞———

Q. Who was the first woman sheriff in Nevada?

A. Clara Dunham Crowell, who took over the post in Lander County in 1919 after her husband George died.

———∞∞∞———

Q. When was the first railroad to Austin completed?

A. The Austin City Railway had its first trial run on May 31, 1881.

———∞∞∞———

Q. What was the name given to the engine of this train?

A. Mules Relief, since the train—not mules any longer—pulled the loads up the steep canyon from the town of Clifton.

Q. When did one of the first recorded railroad wrecks happen in Nevada?

A. About 5:30 P.M. on August 19, 1882, the Mules Relief jumped the tracks about halfway down the canyon into Austin.

Q. How many people were aboard the train, and how many died in the wreck?

A. Only the crew of three were on board. Engineer Andy Wright was killed.

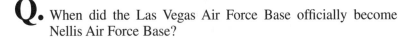

Q. When did the Mules Relief railroad cease operation?

A. 1889.

Q. When did the Las Vegas Air Force Base officially become Nellis Air Force Base?

A. May 1, 1950.

Q. Where did Nellis Air Force Base get its name?

A. It was named after Las Vegas resident Lt. William Harrell Nellis, who died in aerial combat in World War II while flying over Belgium in December 1944.

Q. Where and when did the Air Force Thunderbirds begin?

A. June 26, 1953, at Luke AFB, Arizona.

Q. When were the Thunderbirds transferred to Nellis AFB in Nevada?

A. June 1, 1956.

Q. On what date did a midair collision happen just west of Las Vegas?

A. April 21, 1958, a Nellis AFB jet collided with a United Airlines DC-7, killing 49 people.

Q. The Nevada Central Railway was completed between what Nevada towns?

A. The railroad was completed between Battle Mountain and Austin.

Q. One of western Nevada's largest lakes was discovered and named by what explorer on what date?

A. On January 10, 1844, John C. Fremont discovered and named Pyramid Lake.

Q. A 92-mile narrow-gauge railroad once ran between what Nevada towns?

A. Austin and Battle Mountain.

Q. When was the first airplane flight across the Sierra Nevada that finished with a landing in Carson City?

A. March 22, 1919.

Q. On what date did what president sign the act to organize the Territory of Nevada?

A. The act was signed on March 2, 1861, by President James Buchanan.

Q. By what president, and on what date, was the Walker River Indian Reservation established?

A. The reservation was established by President Ulysses Grant on March 19, 1874.

Q. Since what date has gambling been legal in Nevada?

A. March 19, 1931.

Q. When was the Battle of Pyramid Lake?

A. May 12, 1860.

Q. Who were the opposing factions in this battle?

A. The Paiute Indians, who defeated the white militia.

Q. When did the first automobile cross the Sierra Nevada mountain range?

A. May 27, 1901.

Q. When and where was the first air flight in Nevada?

A. June 23, 1910, at Carson City.

Q. On what date, and by whom, was gold discovered near Virginia City?

A. June 11, 1859, by prospectors Patrick McLaughlin and Peter O'Riley.

Q. When was Clark County established with Las Vegas as the county seat?

A. July 1, 1909.

Q. Who was Nevada's first and only Territorial governor?

A. James Warren Nye.

Q. When did Nye arrive in Carson City to set up the government?

A. July 8, 1861.

Q. Near what Nevada city and on what date did a "mysterious" train derailment kill 24 people?

A. The *City of San Francisco* train derailed west of Elko on August 12, 1939.

Q. What group, on what date, is believed to have robbed the First National Bank of Winnemucca?

A. According to some historical accounts, the Wild Bunch (but without Butch Cassidy and the Sundance Kid) robbed the bank on September 19, 1900.

Q. When was the cornerstone laid for the now historical Federal Building in Carson City?

A. September 29, 1888.

Q. What was the date and location of Nevada's Great Fire?

A. The fire, on October 26, 1875, destroyed most of Virginia City's business district.

Q. On what date and where did the Central Pacific Railroad enter Nevada?

A. December 13, 1867, near the present town of Verdi.

Q. When did John C. Fremont cross the 42nd Parallel and enter for the first time what would become the state of Nevada?

A. December 27, 1843.

Q. When and where did the last stagecoach robbery in Nevada take place?

A. December 5, 1916, in Jarbidge Canyon.

Q. On what date did what discoverer of silver in Virginia City die of frostbite?

A. Ethan Allen, on December 19, 1857.

Q. Who were the famous boxer and lawman who once lived in Tonopah?

A. Jack Dempsey and Wyatt Earp.

Q. Before Tule Springs became a state park, who owned the property?

A. Tule Springs was acquired by the city of Las Vegas and became a city park in the 1960s. Before that time, it was a privately owned popular dude/guest ranch.

Q. What Nevada governor signed the laws to legalize gambling and to set a six-week residency for divorces?

A. Governor Fred Balzar, in 1931.

Q. When and to whom was the first gambling license issued?

A. To Mamie Stocker, on March 20, 1931.

Q. What was the name of her establishment, and where was it located?

A. The Northern Club, at Fremont and Main Streets in Las Vegas.

Q. What was the cost of that first gambling license?

A. $110.00.

Q. Las Vegas was known as what by the railroad?

A. Waterhole No. 25.

Q. What was the first federal building in Nevada?

A. A post office in Carson City, constructed in 1891.

Q. What was the cost of the land for the Governor's Mansion in Carson City?

A. $10.00.

Q. One of Nevada's most publicized hangings took place in what town?

A. Austin.

Q. What was exceptional about the 1868 hanging of Rufus B. Anderson, a convicted murderer?

A. Anderson had to be dropped through the trap three times before he died.

Q. In what year was gambling made illegal in Nevada?

A. 1910.

Q. Why did the legislature outlaw gambling in 1910?

A. A "moral majority–type" group pressured the legislature into making it illegal.

Q. What was the original residency requirement in Nevada for divorces?

A. Six months.

Q. In what year did the legislature change the residency law to 12 months?

A. 1913.

———∞∞∞———

Q. What was the effect of this change on the city of Reno?

A. It caused a major recession!

———∞∞∞———

Q. What did the 1915 legislature do with the divorce residency law?

A. Changed it back to six months.

———∞∞∞———

Q. The 1927 legislature again changed the divorce residency law to what?

A. Ninety days, which remained in effect until 1931, when the six-week law was adopted.

———∞∞∞———

Q. What effect did the 1931 act have on divorces in Nevada?

A. In that year, the number of divorces doubled from 3,000 to 6,000!

———∞∞∞———

Q. What is the waiting period for marriages in Nevada?

A. Marriages can be performed immediately. There is no waiting time or blood test required.

———∞∞∞———

Q. In what year did Raymond "Pappy" Smith open Harold's Club in Reno?

A. 1935.

Q. The legalization of gambling in 1931 brought what reaction from other states?

A. Parts of the country asked for a recall of Nevada's statehood.

Q. What was the intention of the 1931 bill to legalize gambling?

A. To boost Nevada's economy during the Great Depression.

Q. Reno's "red line" law, which restricted casino gambling to the downtown area, was in effect for how long?

A. 1947 to 1972.

Q. Where was Tonopah's first concrete sidewalk?

A. Along the Golden Block, Tonopah's first major commercial development.

Q. Who is the longest-serving member of the state Assembly?

A. Joseph E. Dini Jr. served for 32 years, from 1967 to the present.

Q. Who was the longest-serving female in the state Assembly?

A. Eileen B. Brookman (16 years).

Q. What man served the longest in the state Senate?

A. William F. Dressler (28 years).

Q. What female is the longest-serving member of the state Senate?

A. Ann O'Connell (1985 to the present).

———

Q. Who is the longest-serving man in both the Assembly and Senate?

A. Lawrence E. Jacobsen (Assembly, 1963–1978; Senate, 1980 to the present).

———

Q. Who was the longest-serving female in both houses of the state legislature?

A. Helen Herr (Assembly, 1957–1966; Senate, 1967 to 1976).

———

Q. Who had the longest span of nonconsecutive service in the state legislature?

A. Charles D. Gallagher (first session in 1915, last session in 1964).

———

Q. Who was the youngest female to serve in the state Senate?

A. Helen Foley (age 29; 1983 session).

———

Q. Who was the youngest male to serve in the state Assembly?

A. Richard Kirman (age 21; 1899 session).

———

Q. Who was the only mayor of Las Vegas ever to be elected four consecutive four-year terms?

A. Oran K. Gragson, who served from 1959 until 1975.

ARTS & LITERATURE

C H A P T E R   F O U R

Q. An oil portrait of what famous American was first displayed in the State Capitol in 1915 and was moved to the Assembly Chambers in the new legislative building in 1973?

A. Abraham Lincoln, the so-called Nevada Lincoln portrait.

Q. Who was the artist, and how much was he paid for this work?

A. Charles M. Shean was paid $1,300.

Q. One of the largest art collections in Las Vegas can be found where?

A. In the Bellagio Hotel, which opened in October of 1998.

Q. Who is the Nevada author best known for more than three decades of research and publishing books on virtually every facet of Nevada's history?

A. Stanley W. Paher.

Q. Who is the famed Nevada artist who produced maps and illustrations for many of Paher's works?

A. Roy E. Purcell.

Q. What is the name of the book by Paher that is widely acknowledged as the "bible of Las Vegas history"?

A. *Las Vegas—As It Began—As It Grew.*

Q. What is the name of a well-known female author who was the wife of an equally well-known newspaper editor in Las Vegas?

A. Florence Lee Cahlan, wife of John Cahlan, who along with brother Al, were longtime publishers of the *Las Vegas Review-Journal.*

Q. What is the name of Nevada's largest newspaper?

A. The *Las Vegas Review-Journal.*

Q. What is the name of Nevada's largest, independently owned newspaper?

A. The *Las Vegas Sun.*

Q. Under what special arrangement, approved by the federal government, do these newspapers operate?

A. They have separate and competitive editorial departments, but business functions are combined under a Joint Operating Agreement (JOA).

Q. What was the name of the third daily newspaper in Las Vegas during the late 1970s and early 1980s?

A. The *Valley Times.*

Q. This newspaper ceased publication in 1984 following the death of its owner/publisher. Who was he?

A. Robert Brown, who at one time served as managing editor of the *Review-Journal*.

———∞∞———

Q. What was a major reason for replacing the original Las Vegas city seal on March 16, 1966?

A. The original seal depicted a gushing artesian well, which was symbolic of early Las Vegas. However, after atomic bomb tests began at the nearby Atomic Test Site in the 1950s, many people mistook the artesian well for an atom bomb blast, and objected to it.

———∞∞———

Q. What federal facility occupied the building in Carson City where the Nevada State Museum is located?

A. The U.S. Mint.

———∞∞———

Q. Where is the original State Constitution of Nevada on exhibit?

A. At the Nevada State Library & Archives in Carson City.

———∞∞———

Q. A ranch on the north shore of Lake Tahoe is famed as the site of what western television series?

A. *Bonanza* was filmed at the Ponderosa Ranch.

———∞∞———

Q. What is the name and location of Nevada's oldest museum?

A. The Nevada Historical Society Museum in Reno was founded in 1904.

Q. In what Nevada town is the historic Fourth Ward School?

A. In Virginia City. The school was built in 1876.

Q. What opera house in Nevada is recognized by the League of Historic Theaters as the "most significant vintage theater in the West"?

A. Piper's Opera House in Virginia City, built in the 1880s.

Q. Who was the artist who at age 70 started painting landscapes and became known as the "Grandma Moses of Eldorado Canyon?

A. Bertha Gresch, who came to the Eldorado Canyon in 1904.

Q. Who did the research, writing, photography, and editing for Las Vegas' new city hall dedication brochure in 1973?

A. Kenneth A. Bouton.

Q. What is the name of Nevada's most famous early newspaper?

A. The *Territorial Enterprise*, published in Virginia City.

Q. What famed writer was an early editor of the *Territorial Enterprise* newspaper?

A. Samuel Clemens, better known as Mark Twain.

Q. Who founded what would become Las Vegas' second daily newspaper?

A. Herman "Hank" Greenspun founded the *Las Vegas Sun*.

Q. From what published work is this line taken: "Yessir, you can take it from me. The desert is the place to be."

A. *A Prospector's Prayer*.

Q. What noted photojournalist authored a hardcover book titled *Las Vegas Calling* in 1975?

A. Frank Maggio.

Q. What was the name of Elko's first newspaper and when did it begin publishing?

A. The *Elko Independent* was first issued on June 19, 1869.

Q. In what Nevada town was the University of Nevada first located?

A. Elko.

Q. The location of the first university was open to competition among Nevada cities and counties. Why was Elko chosen over other communities?

A. Elko donated land for the university and also gave $20,000 to help finance it.

Q. On what date did the University of Nevada first open its doors in Elko and to how many students?

A. On October 12, 1874, seven students began attending.

———∞———

Q. When did the university close in Elko, and why?

A. It closed 11 years after it opened, due to declining population.

———∞———

Q. How many students attended the University of Nevada in Elko when it closed?

A. Fifteen.

———∞———

Q. To what other Nevada city was the university moved?

A. Reno, where it has remained.

———∞———

Q. In what year and where was Nevada's first community college established?

A. 1967, in Elko.

———∞———

Q. In what year and where was Nevada's first high school established?

A. 1881, in Elko.

———∞———

Q. Some early Nevada newspapers were actually handwritten. What are the names of two, and the years they were established?

A. The *Golden Canyon Switch*, 1854, and the *Scorpion*, 1857.

Q. What famed southern Nevada artist founded the Las Vegas Art League?

A. Lucile Spire Bruner and a handful of other artists founded the league in 1950.

———∽∾∾∽———

Q. What building in Las Vegas was named in her honor?

A. The Lucile Bruner Elementary School.

———∽∾∾∽———

Q. What former First Lady had some of Bruner's works in her private collection?

A. Nancy Reagan.

———∽∾∾∽———

Q. What was the name of Eureka's first newspaper, and in what year was it founded?

A. The *Eureka Sentinel* began publication in 1870.

———∽∾∾∽———

Q. Who founded and published the *Eureka Sentinel?*

A. Archibald Skillman.

———∽∾∾∽———

Q. In what year did the *Eureka Sentinel* cease publication?

A. 1960.

———∽∾∾∽———

Q. In what year was Eureka's first school built?

A. 1871.

Q. What place in Dayton was a haunt for what famous writer?

A. Mark Twain lived it up in The End of the Trail Saloon, built in the late 1880s.

———⧉———

Q. What was the name of Austin's first newspaper?

A. The *Reese River Reveille.*

———⧉———

Q. When was the *Reveille* established and by whom?

A. W. C. Phillips established the newspaper May 16, 1863.

———⧉———

Q. What historical claim is made by this newspaper?

A. That it is the oldest continuously published newspaper in the state of Nevada.

———⧉———

Q. Reuel Colt Gridley, an Austin merchant, lost a bet concerning Austin's 1864 mayoral election. How did he "pay" the bet?

A. By carrying a 50-pound sack of flour from nearby Clifton to Austin.

———⧉———

Q. How was the "Gridley sack" decorated?

A. With red, white, and blue ribbons, and numerous flags.

———⧉———

Q. How was this event "officially" tied to the town of Austin?

A. Following the town's incorporation in 1864, Morris Locke designed a city seal that commemorated the famous Gridley sack of flour.

Q. Later, an auction of the sack of flour raised donations for the Sanitary Fund, said to be the forerunner of what prominent national organization?

A. The American Red Cross.

⊗⊗⊗

Q. The sack was resold again and again, eventually raising how much money?

A. Over $250,000.

⊗⊗⊗

Q. Who was the former school superintendent, state legislator, and author who wrote books on Nevada history?

A. Dr. R. Guild Gray of Las Vegas, who died in 1998.

⊗⊗⊗

Q. What was the name of an opera singer who grew up in Austin?

A. Emma Wixom, better known as Emma Nevada, who was born in Nevada City, CA, in 1859.

⊗⊗⊗

Q. After she became a famous opera singer, by what nickname was Emma known?

A. The Comstock Nightingale.

⊗⊗⊗

Q. What is the name of a famed history book published in Nevada in 1881?

A. *History of Nevada*, by writers Thompson and West.

Q. Did Austin ever have a daily newspaper?

A. Yes, in the mid-1880s, when the paper was bought by Oscar and Jacob Fairchild, and its name was changed to the *Daily Reese River Reveille*.

Q. What was the name of the editor, and what was the highly popular section of the *Reveille* that was introduced in the 1870s?

A. Editor Fred Hunt started the famous Sazerac Lying Club section, in which the most outlandish stories were printed, with many of these later printed in big city newspapers.

Q. Where did Hunt get the name for this newspaper section?

A. Sazerac was the name of a saloon in Austin, and also the name of a then-popular brandy.

Q. How many other newspapers were published in Austin during the late 1800s?

A. Three.

Q. What were their names and periods of publication?

A. *The Austin Republican*, 1868; *People's Advocate*, December 1890 to January 1893, and *The Daily Morning Democrat*, August 1882 to July 1883.

Q. What was the subscription price of *The Democrat*?

A. $12 per year.

Q. What was the main purpose for establishing *The Democrat*?

A. The paper served as a mouthpiece for the Democratic party and was the foe of the largely Republican *Reveille* and other Republican newspapers throughout the state.

Q. W. W. Booth, founder of *The Democrat* in Austin, later established what other well-known newspaper in what other Nevada town?

A. After starting other newspapers in rural Nevada towns, including Belmont, Booth settled in Tonopah where he ran the *Tonopah Times-Bonanza*.

Q. What was the only newspaper to survive in Austin?

A. The *Reveille*.

Q. Kate St. Clair, one of Nevada's most famed women of all time, was noted for her work in what field?

A. Education, including 15 years of service as State Deputy Superintendent of Public Instruction, beginning in 1944.

Q. During this career, she persuaded the legislature to pass a teachers minimum salary bill, providing minimum annual pay of what amount?

A. $2,400.

Q. How much was St. Clair's salary as a state official?

A. $2,700 a year.

Q. Arthur St. Clair, of Elko, who later would become Kate's husband, received what special honor in education?

A. While attending the University of Nevada in Reno in 1911, he was named Nevada's first Rhodes Scholar, studying at Oxford in England.

Q. What was the name of Las Vegas' first newspaper and what year was it established?

A. The *Las Vegas Age* was established in 1912.

Q. Who was the editor and publisher?

A. Charles P. "Pop" Squires.

Q. What major change in this newspaper took place during the war years?

A. In the 1940s, the *Las Vegas Age* became a Sunday section of the *Las Vegas Review-Journal*.

Q. What Nevada author is claimed to have written the most books under the most names?

A. Jeff Wallman of Reno has authored about 200 books under 20 *noms de plume*.

Q. Cowboy poet Waddie Mitchell was also known by what nickname?

A. Elko's "Poet Lariat."

Q. In what year was the first Cowboy Poetry Gathering in Elko?

A. 1985.

———⬡———

Q. Of the 28 cowboy poets in that gathering, how many were women?

A. Six.

———⬡———

Q. Who was the woman elected to the Nevada legislature in 1946 largely responsible for establishing Nevada University in Las Vegas?

A. Maude Frazier.

———⬡———

Q. In 1962, at the age of 81, Frazier was appointed to what state position?

A. Lieutenant Governor, the highest office in Nevada ever held by a woman.

———⬡———

Q. Who is Nevada's paperback writer whose book sales total more than 20 million copies, in 12 languages?

A. David Eddings.

———⬡———

Q. What is the name of a famed educator/historian/writer from Boulder City?

A. Elbert Edwards.

Q. What is the title of one of his best-known works?

A. *200 Years in Nevada.*

Q. Who was Superintendent of Schools in Boulder City from 1940 to 1963?

A. Elbert Edwards.

Q. Who is the author, and what is the name of, the novel that was later made into a movie with Robert Redford?

A. Norman McLean of Reno wrote *A River Runs Through It.*

Q. Who edited *Desert Wood*, an anthology of Nevada poets?

A. Shaun T. Griffin.

Q. What famed Nevada writer is the son of a Basque sheepherder?

A. Robert Laxalt.

Q. When was the first newspaper established at the Las Vegas Army Air Field, and what was it named?

A. The *Horned Toad* began publication, in mimeograph form, on November 3, 1941.

Q. When was the last issue of the *Horned Toad* published?

A. November 23, 1945.

Q. What was the name and first issue date of the new base newspaper?

A. The *Air Podner* began publication January 18, 1950.

Q. When were actors Ronald Reagan and Burgess Meredith at the Las Vegas Army Air Field to film what movie?

A. July and August of 1942, to film *Tail Gunner*.

Q. Students from what foreign countries were the first to attend the Combat Crew Training Program at the army base?

A. Two Belgian and two French students.

Q. On what date did *Nevada Magazine* begin publication in Carson City?

A. January 2, 1936.

Q. Who was the principal of Virginia City's Fourth Ward School in 1890?

A. John E. Bray.

Q. Where were graduation ceremonies for that school held in 1890?

A. At Piper's Opera House. Two ceremonies were held to accommodate parents who worked different shifts.

Q. What event in Reno in 1940 was attended by many Hollywood stars?

A. The premiere of the movie *Virginia City*.

Q. When did Reno's first newspaper begin publication, and what was it named?

A. *The Reno Crescent* began July 4, 1868.

Q. On what date did what famous writer arrive in Carson City?

A. Samuel Clemens (Mark Twain) arrived there on August 14, 1861.

Q. On what date was what actress born who later worked with Charlie Chaplin?

A. Edna Purviance was born October 21, 1896, in Paradise Valley.

Q. What was Nevada's first commercial radio station, and when and where did it begin broadcasting?

A. Station KOH went on the air in Reno on November 1, 1928.

Q. On what date and where was famed Nevada writer Mark Twain born?

A. Samuel Clemens (Mark Twain) was born November 30, 1835, in Florida, MO.

Q. On what date and where did one of Nevada's most famous newspapers begin publication?

A. On November 3, 1860, the *Territorial Enterprise* began publishing in Virginia City.

———∞———

Q. What Nevada author has an autobiographical work on his World War II–era experiences as a U.S. State Dept. official?

A. Robert Laxalt.

———∞———

Q. What Nevadan is the author of *The Art of Talk*?

A. Art Bell of Pahrump.

———∞———

Q. What U.S. Senator from Nevada has written a book about his hometown?

A. Senator Harry Reid, who authored: *Searchlight: The Camp That Didn't Fail.*

———∞———

Q. What is the title of a late 1990s "how-to" book on gambling?

A. *Knock-Out Blackjack: The Easiest Card-Counting System Ever Devised.*

———∞———

Q. Who wrote this book?

A. Ken Fuchs, an electrical engineer, and Olaf Vancura, a physicist.

Q. A book about the men who made Las Vegas bears what title?

A. *The Players: The Men Who Made Las Vegas*, edited by Jack Sheehan.

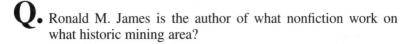

Q. Ronald M. James is the author of what nonfiction work on what historic mining area?

A. *The Road and the Silence: A History of Virginia City and the Comstock Lode.*

Q. Who is the Las Vegas newspaper columnist who has put his favored columns into book form (and what is its title)?

A. John L. Smith, a writer for the *Review-Journal*, wrote *On The Boulevard: The Best of John L. Smith.*

Q. Who is the veteran casino publicist in Las Vegas whose book recalls the Las Vegas of the 1950s, '60s, and '70s?

A. Dick Odessky.

Q. What is the name of Odessky's book?

A. *Fly on the Wall: Recollections of Las Vegas' Good Old, Bad Old Days.*

Q. Who are three of the most noted gaming figures in southern Nevada's history whose "untold stories" are in Odessky's book?

A. Benny Binion, Wilbur Clark, and Howard Hughes, among others.

Q. Who is the one-time Madam of what Nevada brothel who is in the ranks of Nevada's authors?

A. Lora Shaner, who worked at Sheri's Ranch near Pahrump from 1991 to 1996.

Q. What is the title and year of Shaner's book on prostitution?

A. *Madam: Chronicles of a Nevada Cathouse*, published in 1998.

Q. Who is the author and what is the name of the book of special interest to hikers in the southern Nevada area?

A. Branch Whitney wrote *Hiking Las Vegas: 60 Hikes within 60 Minutes of the Strip*.

Q. The works of award-winning poet Gailmarie Pahmeier are featured in what book?

A. *The House on Breakheart Road*.

Q. What are the major awards Pahmeier has received?

A. The Chambers Memorial Award in Poetry, the Witter Bynner Foundation Poetry Fellowship, and two Artists Fellowships from the Nevada State Council of the Arts.

Q. Many newsmen have gone into politics in Nevada. Who is the only former governor who upon leaving office became executive editor of what major daily newspaper?

A. Mike O'Callaghan, governor from 1971 to 1979, is executive editor of the *Las Vegas Sun*.

Q. What is the name of one of the nation's oldest and largest continuously published senior newspapers?

A. The *Nevada Senior World* (which began as *The Rocket* in the mid-1970s).

Q. What was the original name of the Las Vegas newspaper that is now the *Las Vegas Sun*?

A. The *Las Vegas Free Press*.

Q. When did the *Free Press* begin publication, and who was it founded by?

A. The paper started in 1951, founded by the International Typographical Union.

Q. Why did the ITU start the *Free Press*?

A. Printers of the ITU had been "locked out" of the Las Vegas daily newspaper.

Q. The June 21, 1950, edition of the *Free Press* was its first under what new owner/publisher?

A. Hank Greenspun.

Q. What Nevada newswoman is believed to hold the record for serving the most years in the same position for the same newspaper?

A. Ruthe Deskin has served as assistant to the publisher of the *Sun* since 1954.

Q. The history of entertainment in Las Vegas has been recorded on cassettes and CDs by what famed radio personality?

A. Ted Quillin.

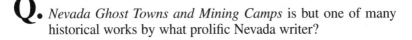

Q. Who wrote *The History of Nevada*?

A. Russell Elliott.

Q. *The Nevada Handbook* was written by what Nevada author?

A. Deke Castleman.

Q. *Nevada Ghost Towns and Mining Camps* is but one of many historical works by what prolific Nevada writer?

A. Stan Paher.

Q. Who is the author of *The Complete Nevada Traveler*?

A. David Toll.

Q. Author Richard Moreno has written what books on travel in northern and southern Nevada?

A. *The Backyard Traveler* (northern Nevada) and *The Backyard Traveler Returns* (southern Nevada).

Q. Upon viewing Lake Tahoe, what famed writer said, "The eye never tired of gazing"?

A. Samuel Clemens, better known as Mark Twain.

Q. Mark Twain's amusing look at life in Nevada in the 1860s is the title of what book?

A. *Roughing It.*

Q. Who is the Nevada cartoonist whose "Pickles" appears in more than 120 newspapers?

A. Brian Crane of Sparks, NV.

Q. Crane's comic strip and a book with the same title are of special interest to what age group?

A. Seniors.

Q. How many graduates were there in Austin's largest-ever senior class?

A. Twelve, in 1987.

Q. What is the name of a military thriller novelist who has written a dozen books to date?

A. Dale Brown, of Incline Village, NV.

Q. Who is Nevada's poet laureate?

A. Norman Kaye.

Q. How long has Kaye held this honorary title, and who appointed him?

A. Kaye has been poet laureate since 1960, when he was appointed by then-governor Grant Sawyer.

———⊗⊗⊗———

Q. During the "big name" era of entertainment in Las Vegas resorts, Kaye was famed as what?

A. A member of the Mary Kaye Trio, one of the Strip's most popular singing groups.

———⊗⊗⊗———

Q. What is the name of a Nevada patriotic song written by Kaye?

A. "Hail to Nevada."

———⊗⊗⊗———

Q. What is the name of the poem written by Kaye in 1960 that became the national song for the March of Dimes?

A. "Throw a Dime My Way."

———⊗⊗⊗———

Q. What famed writer described a view of Nevada as "...the loveliest picture with which the hand of the Creator has adorned the earth, according to the best of my knowledge and belief, so help me God"?

A. Mark Twain, in 1863.

———⊗⊗⊗———

Q. What is the title of the book written in 1976 by David Beatty and Robert O. Beatty?

A. *Nevada, Land of Discovery.*

Q. What is the name of the book, and its author, that looks at religion on the Comstock?

A. *Nevada's Bonanza Church: St. Mary's in the Mountains*, by Virgil A. Bucchianeri.

Q. A Utah writer has also written a book about religion in Virginia City. What is her name and the title of her work?

A. Anne M. Butler wrote *Mission in the Mountains: The Daughters of Charity in Virginia City*.

Q. What is the title of a Nevada University Press release that also tells about the role of women in Virginia City's early history?

A. *Comstock Women: The Making of a Mining Community*.

Q. Who is said to be Nevada's first female historian?

A. Laura M. Ellis Dettenrieder.

Q. Laura and her husband arrived by covered wagon in what Nevada town and what year?

A. Dayton, in 1853.

Q. What is the earliest known published account of her work?

A. *Thompson & West*, published in 1881.

Q. She is also mentioned in what other early records?

A. A history of Dayton published by the Nevada Historical Society in 1922.

———— ∞ ————

Q. Where can one find what is claimed to be the largest collection of Indian artifacts and western art in Nevada?

A. The Wigwam Restaurant in Fernley.

———— ∞ ————

Q. Clark Gable and Marilyn Monroe made what movie in what Nevada town?

A. *The Misfits* was filmed in Dayton.

———— ∞ ————

Q. In what year did Edna Purviance begin her Hollywood acting career with Chaplin?

A. 1915.

———— ∞ ————

Q. In how many films did she have a starring role with Chaplin?

A. Thirty-five.

———— ∞ ————

Q. What famed artist lived in Pahrump the last 15 years of his life?

A. Lew Flyge.

———— ∞ ————

Q. What are some of the major companies whose packages Flyge designed?

A. C & H Sugar, Morton's Salt, Mother's Cookies, Paul Masson Wines.

Q. In his later years, Flyge became famed for what?

A. His southwestern desert landscapes.

———∞———

Q. Art Bell's nationally famous radio talk show originates in what Nevada town?

A. Pahrump.

———∞———

Q. The *Times*, the *Self-Cocker*, and the *Tarantula* were names of short-lived newspapers in what old mining camp?

A. Belleville.

———∞———

Q. Where did Samuel Clemens (Mark Twain) work as a miner before he was hired as a reporter for the *Virginia City Enterprise*?

A. The old town of Aurora; he worked there one week in 1882.

———∞———

Q. What were the names of the two newspapers in Aurora in 1863?

A. The semiweekly *Esmeralda Star* and the daily *Times*.

———∞———

Q. What was the name of another newspaper in Aurora in early 1906?

A. The *Aurora Borealis*, a weekly.

———∞———

Q. What female reporter for what Nevada newspaper has written the most articles about operations at the Nevada Test Site?

A. Mary Manning, during more than 30 years at the *Las Vegas Sun* newspaper.

SPORTS & LEISURE

C H A P T E R   F I V E

Q. What is the name of Nevada's only national park, and when was it established?

A. Great Basin National Park, established in 1987.

———❦———

Q. What is the only small town in Nevada served by Amtrak?

A. Caliente.

———❦———

Q. Caliente is the site of what "natural" tourist attraction?

A. Its hot springs.

———❦———

Q. Where is the Loneliest Road in America?

A. A 287-mile stretch of U.S. Hwy. 50, east-west across Nevada.

———❦———

Q. What is the origin of the "loneliest road" designation?

A. An article in *Life Magazine*, July 1986.

Q. Why was this road so named by the magazine?

A. According to the article, there "are no attractions or points of interest," and motorists needed "survival skills" to travel the route.

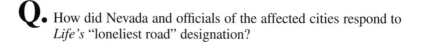

Q. How did Nevada and officials of the affected cities respond to *Life's* "loneliest road" designation?

A. The Nevada State legislature officially designated this route as the "loneliest road," and thousands of "survival kits" containing road maps and other tourist information have been distributed in towns along the route.

Q. To facilitate tourist promotion, Nevada has been divided into six geographic territories. What are their names?

A. The Reno-Tahoe, Las Vegas, Pioneer, Pony Express, Cowboy Country, and Indian territories.

Q. The town of Elko, in Cowboy Country, holds a nationally recognized annual nonrodeo event for cowboys. What is the event?

A. The Cowboy Poetry Gathering.

Q. The town of Tonopah, in Pioneer Territory, is famed for what annual event?

A. Its Jim Butler Days, featuring a variety of mining-related contests and events, is named after one of Tonopah's settlers.

Q. Many Nevada settlers came from a certain area in Spain. What annual festival in what Nevada city pays tribute to these pioneers?

A. The Winnemucca Basque Festival.

Q. Ripley's *Believe It Or Not* featured the depot in the historic ghost town of Rhyolite. Why?

A. Though the depot was a magnificent structure for its day, the town closed in 1910—before the railroad tracks were laid!

Q. In addition to the loneliest Road in America, Nevada has another state route that has attracted worldwide attention. What is the name of this road?

A. The Extraterrestrial Highway.

Q. Where is this route, and why is it so-named?

A. A 98-mile stretch of S.R. 375 runs near the Air Force's top-secret Area 51. The route has long been a gathering place for UFO enthusiasts, and according to reports, more UFOs have been sighted in this area than anywhere else in the world.

Q. Where is the Ruby Marsh Recreational Area?

A. In Elko County, south of the city of Elko.

Q. Where are the Nevada State Cowboy Action Shooting Championships held?

A. In the towns of Pahrump and Beatty.

Q. Where is the annual Mother Earth Awakening Pow Wow held?

A. Carson City.

———⊗⊗⊗———

Q. The Spring Jamboree and Crafts Fair, one of the state's largest, is held where?

A. In Boulder City.

———⊗⊗⊗———

Q. What is the name of Las Vegas' largest enclosed sports arena?

A. The Thomas & Mack Center.

———⊗⊗⊗———

Q. What is the name of Las Vegas' largest outdoor sports facility?

A. The Sam Boyd Silver Bowl.

———⊗⊗⊗———

Q. Las Vegas is the home of what internationally famed tennis player?

A. Andre Agassi.

———⊗⊗⊗———

Q. In what year did the Runnin' Rebels (University of Nevada, Las Vegas) basketball team win the national championship?

A. 1990.

———⊗⊗⊗———

Q. On what lake are Formula One Hydroplane races held?

A. Lake Mead.

Q. In what "liveliest ghost town in the West" are camel races held?

A. Virginia City.

———∞∞∞———

Q. Where are the world's largest National Championship Air Races held?

A. Reno, at Stead Airport.

———∞∞∞———

Q. What town hosts the annual Harvest Festival, Parade, and Rodeo?

A. Pahrump.

———∞∞∞———

Q. Where is the annual Pine Nut Festival held?

A. The town of Schurz, on the Walker River Indian Reservation.

———∞∞∞———

Q. What city hosts the World Championship Chili Cook-Off?

A. Reno.

———∞∞∞———

Q. What is the longest vehicle race in Nevada?

A. The 546-mile Best in the Desert/Las Vegas to Reno Adventure.

———∞∞∞———

Q. What record-setting event occurred at the Palace Station Casino in Las Vegas on November 15, 1998?

A. A Las Vegas woman won $27,582,539.48 while playing a Megabucks jackpot.

Q. In the previous month, on the day her husband retired, this same woman hit a jackpot in what amount?

A. $689,000!

———∞———

Q. There are Megabucks slot machines in how many Nevada casinos?

A. About 133 casinos have these machines, which are all linked together.

———∞———

Q. What is the minimum amount a player must spend to have a chance to win the Megabucks jackpot?

A. $3.00.

———∞———

Q. How many times has the Megabucks jackpot been hit?

A. Forty-seven.

———∞———

Q. How many times has the Megabucks jackpot topped $8 million?

A. Ten.

———∞———

Q. Including the record win on November 15, 1998, what is the total amount paid out on Megabucks jackpots?

A. About $246 million.

———∞———

Q. In what Nevada town are burro races the feature of the town's annual festival?

A. The Great Burro Races are held in Beatty.

Q. One of Nevada's legal annual holidays also falls on the same date as a national observance of what day?

A. The anniversary of statehood in Carson City each October 31, which is also Halloween.

Q. Name Nevada's four best-known "ghost towns."

A. Rhyolite, Belmont, Berlin, and Tuscarora.

Q. What is the town founded in 1865 that remains Nevada's oldest and largest "living ghost town"?

A. Belmont.

Q. What is the only operating business in Belmont today?

A. The town is dotted with historic ruins, including the old court house, but the only active business is a saloon, where a historic backbar and other artifacts are on display.

Q. Which Nevada ghost town is considered the state's most photogenic?

A. Rhyolite, near Death Valley National Park.

Q. What major sports event took place in Carson City in 1892?

A. Bob Fitzsimmons defeated James J. Corbett in a heavyweight championship fight.

Q. When and where was the first supersonic land speed record set?

A. October 15, 1997, in Nevada's Black Rock Desert.

───⊗───

Q. Who did the UNLV Rebels defeat to win the 1990 NCAA Division 1 basketball championship, and what was the score?

A. The Rebels defeated Duke by a score of 103 to 73.

───⊗───

Q. Who coached UNLV's 1990 championship team?

A. Jerry Tarkanian.

───⊗───

Q. Who received the John R. Wooden award as the nation's outstanding college basketball player in 1991?

A. Larry Johnson, of the University of Nevada, Las Vegas.

───⊗───

Q. For what is Nevada's Berlin-Ichthyosaur State Park most noted?

A. Nevada's state fossil, the *ichthyosaur*, a giant fish-lizard, is preserved in stone in this park.

───⊗───

Q. What is the area of Walker Lake, and what is it known for?

A. The 36,000-acre lake is noted for cutthroat trout fishing and all types of water sports.

───⊗───

Q. Where is the longest nine-hole golf course in Nevada?

A. The Round Mountain Golf Club, about 60 miles north of Tonopah.

Q. A four-sport standout who was born in Tonopah in 1912 and died in Reno in 1938 was known as Nevada's Greatest Forgotten Athlete. Who was he?

A. Jack Hill, who excelled in football, baseball, basketball, and track, and whose name is in Nevada's Hall of Fame.

———— ✺ ————

Q. At what Las Vegas hotel was the Miss Rodeo America pageant held in 1970?

A. The Frontier.

———— ✺ ————

Q. Who won the title?

A. Miss Rodeo California, Christine Vincent from Clovis, CA, went on to earn the national title for 1970.

———— ✺ ————

Q. Who was the motion picture cowboy that helped stage this event?

A. Chill Wills.

———— ✺ ————

Q. On what nearby mountain is year-round recreation available to residents of the Las Vegas area?

A. Mt. Charleston, which offers a full array of both winter and summer recreational activities.

———— ✺ ————

Q. Lake Mead, created by the construction of Hoover Dam on the Colorado River, was named in honor of whom?

A. Dr. Elwood Mead, U.S. Commissioner of Reclamation from 1924 to 1936.

Q. What is Lake Mead noted for?

A. Year-round water sports of all kinds.

———❦———

Q. Where does the water in Pahranagat Lake come from?

A. The run-off from Ash Springs.

———❦———

Q. Where is Pahranagat Lake?

A. Along the west side of U.S. 92, about seven miles south of the town of Alamo.

———❦———

Q. How many state parks are located within 50 miles of Caliente?

A. Five, three of which have reservoirs for boating.

———❦———

Q. What is the name of a prominent historic state monument near Ely?

A. The Ward charcoal ovens are 11 miles south of Ely and easily accessible by any vehicle.

———❦———

Q. What is the name and location of one of the most photographed churches in America?

A. The Lamoille Presbyterian Church, about 20 miles southeast of Elko.

———❦———

Q. In what year was the Lamoille Canyon area declared a U.S. Scenic Area?

A. 1965.

Q. Lamoille Canyon forms a crescent in what mountain range?

A. The Ruby Mountains in northern Nevada.

Q. What is the highest elevation accessible by car in these mountains?

A. 8,800 feet.

Q. What is special about skiing in the Ruby Mountains?

A. Skiers are transported to the top of the runs by helicopter.

Q. The Ruby Mountains are home to what wildlife?

A. Mountain lions, bighorn sheep, mountain goats, deer, and elk.

Q. When was the first paved road constructed into Lamoille Canyon?

A. 1942.

Q. What U.S. highway in Nevada is known as The Great Basin Highway?

A. U.S. 93.

Q. Why was Jackpot built?

A. The town was built only for gambling.

Q. What famous boxer of the 1920s once worked as a bouncer in bars in what Nevada town?

A. Jack Dempsey, in Wells.

Q. Where can you visit a drugstore filled with products and pharmaceutical records from as early as 1915?

A. The McGill Drug Store, in McGill, which closed in 1980, was donated to the White Pine Public Museum in 1995.

Q. What town claims to be the home of the best preserved rail yard in the U.S.?

A. Ely.

Q. What are the major attractions at the old rail yard in Ely?

A. Two old steam engines from the early 1900s and an antique diesel engine.

Q. In addition to "looking," what else can railroad buffs do in Ely?

A. The "Ghost Train" offers scheduled passenger runs up historic Robinson Canyon to the Keystone Junction near the town of Ruth.

Q. What area of Nevada is noted for an abundance of wildflowers and Monarch butterflies?

A. The Ely area.

Q. The archaeological site of the Fremont People, an ancient Indian tribe, is located near what Nevada town?

A. Baker, at the east entrance to Great Basin National Park.

———

Q. What fish is one of the rarest Nevada species?

A. The bull trout.

———

Q. When is "free fishing day" in Nevada, when no license is required?

A. The second Saturday in June of each year.

———

Q. Do Nevada senior citizens get a discount on fishing and hunting licenses?

A. Persons age 65 and older who have continuously resided in Nevada at least five years are charged $8.00 for a combination fishing and hunting license.

———

Q. Upon meeting qualifications, what adult residents are granted free licenses?

A. Disabled veterans and Native Americans.

———

Q. For ice fishing, what is the maximum diameter of the hole in the ice?

A. Ten inches.

———

Q. What are Nevada's two most popular fishing areas?

A. Lakes Mead and Mohave, both on the Colorado River.

Q. Is fishing available in the Las Vegas metro area?

A. Yes, in ponds at Sunset Park, Lorenzi Park, and Floyd Lamb State Park.

Q. How many wildlife management areas (WMA) are there in Nevada?

A. Seven.

Q. In what year was the Nevada Wildlife Commission established?

A. 1877.

Q. The Northeastern Nevada Museum is required to "pay rent" on a relic on display in the museum. What is the relic?

A. The old saloon bar from Halleck.

Q. In what very unique form does the museum pay rent for this display?

A. The annual rent is paid in the form of one bottle of Beefeater's Gin, served over the bar during an invitation-only affair.

Q. The museum's traveling show of what works is claimed to be the most visited art exhibit in the state?

A. The annual traveling show of Nevada photography.

Q. Elko's Convention Center opened with a concert by what group?

A. The Utah Symphony Orchestra.

Q. Name two performers who have drawn standing-room-only crowds at the Convention Center?

A. Wolfman Jack and Willie Nelson.

———⸎———

Q. In the late 1800s, what hotel advertised as the "only fire-proof hotel in Nevada"?

A. The Jackson House in Eureka, after it was rebuilt following a disastrous fire.

———⸎———

Q. In what year did the famed Jackson House become the Brown Hotel?

A. 1907.

———⸎———

Q. After many years of vacancy, this structure was restored as a historical building in what year?

A. 1981.

———⸎———

Q. By what name is this building known today, and what is its use?

A. Again it is known as the Jackson House, and it operates as a bar and hotel.

———⸎———

Q. What Eureka structure is arguably the town's most noted landmark?

A. The Eureka Opera House.

Q. When was the Eureka Opera House built?

A. In late 1880, on the foundation of the Odd Fellows Hall, which was destroyed by fire in August 1879.

———∞∞———

Q. In what year did the Eureka Opera House receive a National Preservation Honor award?

A. 1944.

———∞∞———

Q. Is prostitution "legal" everywhere in Nevada?

A. No. But houses of prostitution are "tolerated" in many of Nevada's rural areas.

———∞∞———

Q. Is prostitution prohibited by law anywhere in Nevada?

A. Yes. By local and/or county law, prostitution is illegal in Nevada's major population centers of Las Vegas (Clark County), Reno (Washoe County), and in rural Lincoln County.

———∞∞———

Q. What is the "universal" sign of prostitution in Nevada's rural communities?

A. Flashing red lights identify the bawdy houses.

———∞∞———

Q. What Nevada city welcomes tourists with an archway sign over its main street?

A. Reno.

Q. What were the original words of greeting on the arch, and when was Reno's first arch installed?

A. "Reno Transcontinental Highway Exposition" appeared on the first arch, installed in 1926.

Q. What slogan was on the new Reno arch erected in 1929?

A. "Biggest Little City in the World."

Q. When and by whom was a large area of Nevada closed to hunters?

A. On September 29, 1961, the Nevada Fish and Game Commission closed the Belted Range at the request of Nellis AFB and the Atomic Energy Commission.

Q. When did the Air Force transfer the Mt. Charleston Recreation Area to the forest service?

A. April 10, 1963.

Q. When and where did the Corbett-Fitzsimmons heavyweight championship fight take place?

A. March 17, 1897, in Carson City.

Q. Who won the championship?

A. Robert Fitzsimmons.

Q. When and where did Leon Spinks defeat Muhammad Ali?

A. February 15, 1978, in Las Vegas.

Q. On November 22, 1986, what championship fight was in Las Vegas?

A. Mike Tyson KO'd Trevor Berbick.

Q. Who did Mike Tyson defeat in a March 7, 1987 fight in Las Vegas?

A. James "Bonecrusher" Smith.

Q. Who fought in Las Vegas on May 30, 1987?

A. Tony Tucker KO'd James Douglas.

Q. Tucker was defeated in Las Vegas when and by whom?

A. August 1, 1987, by Mike Tyson.

Q. Who were the fighters in an October 25, 1990 fight in Las Vegas?

A. Evander Holyfield KO'd James Douglas.

Q. When did Riddick Bowe defeat Holyfield in Las Vegas?

A. November 13, 1992.

Q. Who fought in a championship bout in what central Nevada town in 1906?

A. The Gans-Nelson fight was in Goldfield on September 3 of that year.

Q. The daughter of what Nevada congressman married what Hall of Fame baseball star on June 24, 1914?

A. Cong. E. E. Roberts' daughter married Walter "Big Train" Johnson.

Q. What is the name and location of Nevada's newest state park?

A. Big Bend, on the shores of the Colorado River, five miles south of Laughlin.

Q. How high can summer temperatures reach at Big Bend?

A. One hundred twenty degrees, or higher!

Q. How many state parks and/or state recreational areas are there in Nevada?

A. Twenty-four.

Q. Who built the first complete tennis facility in Las Vegas?

A. Wilbur Clark, owner of the Desert Inn.

Q. What was Las Vegas' first major sporting event?

A. The Tournament of Champions, played at the Desert Inn's 18-hole golf course.

Q. What was the first prize awarded at this tournament?

A. A wheelbarrow filled with newly minted silver dollars.

———— ✼ ————

Q. Who was the boxing great who won his only fight in Las Vegas?

A. Archie Moore, who died December 9, 1998, in San Diego at age 84.

———— ✼ ————

Q. When and who did Moore fight in Las Vegas?

A. On May 2, 1955, Moore took a 15-round decision over Nino Valdez.

———— ✼ ————

Q. Where was this fight held?

A. At the old Cashman Field.

———— ✼ ————

Q. Moore also worked in Las Vegas as a trainer for what heavyweight champion?

A. George Foreman.

———— ✼ ————

Q. North America's largest concentration of ski areas is located where?

A. There are 11 ski areas in the Tahoe Basin.

———— ✼ ————

Q. How many year-round golf courses are within an hour's drive of Carson City?

A. Six.

Q. Which one of these is considered one of the West's top golf courses?

A. The Golf Club at Genoa Lakes.

———⸄⸅———

Q. Opened in September of 1996, the Las Vegas Motor Speedway sold in December 1998 for how much money?

A. A reported $215 million.

———⸄⸅———

Q. Who were the original co-owners of the Speedway?

A. Las Vegas hotel magnates Ralph Englestad and Bill Bennett.

———⸄⸅———

Q. What is the seating capacity at the Speedway?

A. One hundred seven thousand.

———⸄⸅———

Q. What was the largest crowd ever to see a sporting event in Nevada, and what was that event?

A. The Winston Cup race in March of 1989 was attended by 135,000 fans.

———⸄⸅———

Q. What heavyweight title bout in Las Vegas on what date brought a fine and suspension for one of the fighters' licenses?

A. The June 28, 1997, match between Mike Tyson and Evander Holyfield.

Q. Which fighter was fined and had his license suspended, and for what reason?

A. Tyson was suspended for 15 months for biting the ears of Holyfield.

———∞———

Q. What action did the Nevada Athletic Commission take at the end of Tyson's license suspension?

A. The commission reissued Tyson's license.

———∞———

Q. Back Alley Fights, featuring professional boxers, is an annual celebration held in what Nevada town?

A. Yerington.

———∞———

Q. In what year was Walley's Hot Springs resort opened in Genoa?

A. 1862.

———∞———

Q. In what year was the Carson Hot Springs resort established?

A. 1849.

———∞———

Q. How many public RV campgrounds are in Nevada's Pony Express territory?

A. Thirty.

———∞———

Q. How many golf courses are there in the Las Vegas area?

A. Twenty-nine at the end of 1998; several more are planned.

SCIENCE & NATURE

C H A P T E R   S I X

Q. What percentage of the nation's gold, and what percentage of the world's total output of gold, respectively, come from Nevada mines?

A. Sixty-six and one-half percent of the nation's gold, and 10 percent of the world's total output.

—————

Q. How much of Nevada's total land area is directly affected by mining?

A. About one-tenth of one percent, according to the Nevada Mining Association.

—————

Q. What is considered to be Nevada's first major industry?

A. Mining: gold, silver, lead, and many other minerals.

—————

Q. When and where was the first ore mill built in Nevada?

A. In 1860 an ore mill was built at Galena to process gold from the Comstock Lode.

Q. When and where were some of the first lead deposits discovered in Nevada?

A. In 1856, lead was discovered in the Spring Mountains just west of Las Vegas.

———— ✿ ————

Q. In what year was the famed Eureka silver-lead district discovered?

A. In 1862, in the Reese River area near the town of Austin.

———— ✿ ————

Q. In 1873, Nevada became the world leader in the production of what mineral?

A. Borax, from the plant at Teels Marsh.

———— ✿ ————

Q. The year 1878 saw the completion of what major mining project in Nevada?

A. Completion of the Sutro Tunnel at the 1,640-foot level of the Savage Mine in Virginia City brought in a new era of activity at the Comstock Lode.

———— ✿ ————

Q. How many precious metal (gold and silver) mines are operating in Nevada?

A. More than 38 major mining operations were underway in the late 1990s.

———— ✿ ————

Q. In the late 1990s, Nevada had how many oil-producing wells?

A. More than 35, according to the Nevada Mining Association.

Q. How many geothermal energy plants for the generation of electricity operate in Nevada?

A. There were 14 operating plants in the late 1990s.

———————∞———————

Q. In addition to precious metal mines, how many other industrial and mineral mines were there in Nevada in the late 1990s?

A. More than two dozen such mines operate throughout the state.

———————∞———————

Q. The site of rich gold deposits found by Harry Stimler and William Marsh in 1902 later became what town in Nevada?

A. Goldfield.

———————∞———————

Q. In what year did the first copper production come from mines near Ely?

A. Major copper production from mines near Ely and in White Pine Canyon began in 1907.

———————∞———————

Q. The discovery of gold at Weepah in what year triggered a major milestone in Nevada's mining history?

A. The last gold rush in Nevada took place in 1927 as a result of this gold strike.

———————∞———————

Q. How much money has been invested in mining explorations, building, and equipment for plants since 1980?

A. More than $10 billion, according to the Nevada Mining Association.

Q. In what year did Nevada become the nation's leading producer of Tungsten?

A. 1946.

―――∞∞∞―――

Q. The year 1951 saw what major development in the Nevada mining industry?

A. The first substantial production of iron ore in Nevada mines began that year.

―――∞∞∞―――

Q. The first major shipment of copper concentrate from Anaconda's Yerington mine occurred in what year?

A. 1953.

―――∞∞∞―――

Q. What gold discovery in 1962 contains more than 20 mines and is now one of the world's largest gold-producing regions?

A. The Carlin Trend in northern Nevada, whose gold reserves are said to exceed 100 million ounces of gold.

―――∞∞∞―――

Q. In 1965, Nevada was ranked first in the United States in production of what mineral?

A. Barite.

―――∞∞∞―――

Q. The Newmont Gold Company, one of the world's largest mining operations, was formerly known by what name?

A. The Carlin Gold Company.

Q. In what year, and in what area, did the Smoky Valley Mining Company begin production?

A. The Round Mountain Mine in Nye County in central Nevada began production of gold in 1977.

———⚬⚬⚬———

Q. What southern Nevada city is the home of what well-known mining school?

A. The McCaw School of Mines opened in Henderson in 1966. The school features simulated open pit and underground mine structures, and students learn about mining history and hands-on earth science.

———⚬⚬⚬———

Q. For the fifth year in a row, Nevada's gold mines have collectively produced how much gold?

A. More than six million ounces each year, making Nevada the largest gold producing state in the nation with nearly two-thirds of all gold production.

———⚬⚬⚬———

Q. The American Society of Civil Engineers in 1955 gave what recognition to Hoover Dam?

A. The dam was selected as one of America's seven modern civil engineering wonders.

———⚬⚬⚬———

Q. On what date and to what company was the contract for the construction of Hoover Dam awarded?

A. The contract for construction of the dam was awarded to Six Companies on March 11, 1932, and "notice to proceed" was given on April 20.

Q. When was the first concrete poured for Hoover Dam? When was the last?

A. June 6, 1933, and May 29, 1935.

———— ❧ ————

Q. When did the generation of electricity begin at Hoover Dam?

A. October 26, 1936.

———— ❧ ————

Q. From 1939 to 1949, Hoover Dam was the largest hydroelectric facility in the world. Its generating capacity was surpassed by what dam?

A. The Grand Coulee Dam.

———— ❧ ————

Q. When did record-high Colorado River runoffs fill Lake Mead to capacity, with water overflowing the top of raised spillway gates at Hoover Dam?

A. This event, in the late evening of July 2, 1983, was the first "spill" since 1941.

———— ❧ ————

Q. How many men were employed during the construction of Hoover Dam?

A. An average of 3,500 people, with a maximum of 5,218 which occurred in June 1934.

———— ❧ ————

Q. What was the average monthly payroll during construction of Hoover Dam?

A. $500,000.

Q. Where did the electrical power needed for construction of Hoover Dam come from?

A. A 222-mile-long power transmission line from San Bernardino, CA, was built for this purpose.

———⊶⊷———

Q. What is the tallest building west of the Mississippi?

A. The Stratosphere Tower in Las Vegas at 1,149 feet.

———⊶⊷———

Q. What other height record is claimed by the Stratosphere Tower?

A. It is claimed to be the tallest free-standing observation tower in the U.S.

———⊶⊷———

Q. How fast do the elevators in the Stratosphere Tower travel?

A. Eighteen hundred feet per minute.

———⊶⊷———

Q. How long does it take for the Stratosphere Tower elevator to travel from the ground to the observation decks?

A. Thirty seconds.

———⊶⊷———

Q. The Stratosphere Tower's High Roller roller coaster is claimed to be the world's highest roller coaster. How high is it?

A. More than 100 stories above the ground.

———⊶⊷———

Q. Nevada leads the nation in the production of gold, and in what other metal?

A. Nevada also produces more silver than any other state.

Q. Representatives from seven states and the federal government convened in 1922 for what historical purpose?

A. To establish the Colorado River Compact.

———∞———

Q. When was this document signed, and what was its purpose?

A. Signed November 24, 1922, in Santa Fe, NM, the compact divided the Colorado River into an upper and lower basin, and gave half the river's estimated annual flow to each basin.

———∞———

Q. This compact provided how many acre-feet of Colorado River annually to Nevada?

A. About 300,000 acre-feet.

———∞———

Q. An acre-foot of water equals how many gallons?

A. About 326,000.

———∞———

Q. When did the last electrical generating unit go on-line at Hoover Dam?

A. December 1, 1961.

———∞———

Q. On what date in 1963 was Hoover Dam closed to visitors for one day?

A. November 25, to mourn the death of President John F. Kennedy.

Q. What was the amount of the construction contract for Hoover Dam?

A. $48,890,995.

―――∞∞∞―――

Q. How much concrete is in Hoover Dam?

A. There are 4,360,000 cubic yards of concrete in the dam, power plant, and appurtenant works.

―――∞∞∞―――

Q. If this amount of concrete was poured into a monument 100 feet square, how tall would it be?

A. Two and one-half miles.

―――∞∞∞―――

Q. How long would a 16-foot-wide highway extend if it were built from the concrete in Hoover Dam?

A. The highway would extend from San Francisco to New York City.

―――∞∞∞―――

Q. How was the heat generated by setting concrete in the dam dissipated?

A. By pumping ice water through more than 582 miles of one-inch steel pipe embedded in the structure.

―――∞∞∞―――

Q. How high is Hoover Dam and how much does it weigh?

A. It is 726.4 feet and more than 6,600,000 tons.

Q. How many miles of railroad track were laid to build Hoover Dam?

A. From the Union Pacific main line in Las Vegas to Boulder City, 22.7 miles of standard-gauge track, and an additional 10 miles from Boulder City to the dam site.

———∞———

Q. At elevation 1,221.4 feet, how much water does Lake Mead hold?

A. 28,537,000 acre-feet.

———∞———

Q. How many intake towers supply water for the power plant turbines at the dam?

A. Four.

———∞———

Q. What are the dimensions of the intake towers?

A. Each tower is 395 feet high, with a diameter of 82 feet at the base, 63 feet, 3 inches at the top.

———∞———

Q. What was Nevada's Tonopah Test Range Airfield noted for in the early 1990s?

A. Training for Air Force pilots of the F-117A fighter plane.

———∞———

Q. What Nevada town is known as The Greatest Gold Camp on Earth?

A. Goldfield.

———∞———

Q. What is the name of a major scientific facility in Tonopah?

A. The Tonopah Aeronautical and Technology Park.

Q. What is the average annual rainfall in Tonopah?

A. 5.32 inches.

———∞∞∞———

Q. What is the average high temperature in Tonopah in July?

A. 91.0°F.

———∞∞∞———

Q. What is the average low temperature in Tonopah in January?

A. 18.1°F.

———∞∞∞———

Q. Near what Nevada town do Sandhill cranes gather for a break in their southward migration in the fall and their northward migration in the spring?

A. Lund.

———∞∞∞———

Q. What mining town became known as The Widow Maker, and why?

A. Delamar. Dry-milling processes created a silicone, or "death dust," which is said to have caused the deaths of many workers.

———∞∞∞———

Q. How did the town of Hiko get its name?

A. The word is an Indian expression for "white man's town."

———∞∞∞———

Q. What southern Nevada town was created solely to support America's defense?

A. Henderson.

Q. Why was Henderson vital to the war effort, and why has it remained vital to the nation's space programs and other scientific endeavors?

A. For its production of magnesium for munitions, aircraft parts, and many other industrial uses.

———✷———

Q. Nevada's first successful shale oil distribution plant was located in what town?

A. Elko.

———✷———

Q. In what area of Nevada were coal deposits found in 1861?

A. In Eldorado Canyon, southeast of Dayton.

———✷———

Q. What size claims were allowed in the new coal mining district?

A. Forty acres in each claim.

———✷———

Q. In what other areas of western Nevada has coal been found?

A. Near Walker Lake, and in the Washoe Valley.

———✷———

Q. In the 1860s a toll bridge was built over what river in Nevada?

A. The Boliver Toll Bridge (named after its builder) spanned the Carson River at Dayton.

———✷———

Q. When did this toll bridge cease operating, and why?

A. In the late 1800s, it was flooded out.

Q. When and where in Nevada was one of North America's most important archaeological discoveries?

A. In 1940, the oldest mummified remains of man on the continent were discovered in a cave in the Grimes Point area, east of Fallon.

Q. By what name are the mummified remains known in scientific circles?

A. Spirit Cave Man.

Q. How long ago was Spirit Cave Man buried?

A. An estimated 9,415 years.

Q. Who discovered Spirit Cave Man?

A. S. M. and Georgia Wheeler.

Q. What government agency has possession of Spirit Cave Man?

A. The Nevada Museums and History Division.

Q. Other ancient remains of man were discovered at Pyramid Lake. How old are these remains, and by what name are they known?

A. The remains of Wizards Beach Man are 9,225 years old.

Q. Although Las Vegas is in the Pacific Standard time zone, some northeastern Nevada towns farther west than Las Vegas are on what time?

A. Mountain Standard Time.

Q. What was the Austin-Manhattan project near Austin?

A. A 6,000-foot drainage tunnel into Lander Hill to drain excess water from mines.

Q. Who was the first woman physician in Nevada?

A. Dr. Eliza Cook (1856–1947), who practiced medicine in the Carson Valley for 40 years.

Q. When was the first military air landing in Las Vegas?

A. April 29, 1930, at the Western Air Express Field just outside of Las Vegas.

Q. When did the Army and the city of Las Vegas sign a lease for the Army Air Field, on land that the city had purchased from Western Air Express for $10?

A. January 25, 1941.

Q. When was the first fire department for the new army airfield established?

A. July 7, 1941.

Q. What equipment did the fire department have when it first opened?

A. A 1918 Ford Model T fire truck that had to be pushed wherever it went!

———⊗⊗⊗———

Q. When did the first training squadrons arrive?

A. July 7–12, 1941.

———⊗⊗⊗———

Q. When was the Tonopah Bombing Range established?

A. August 25, 1941.

———⊗⊗⊗———

Q. How large was this facility when established?

A. 983,040 acres.

———⊗⊗⊗———

Q. When did the Atomic Energy Commission detonate Nevada's first above-ground atomic test?

A. January 27, 1951.

———⊗⊗⊗———

Q. How powerful was the atomic bomb detonation on November 23, 1951?

A. It was seen in Salt Lake City, 450 miles northeast of the blast site, and felt in Phoenix, 400 miles southeast.

Q. In what year were large bodies of silver discovered in Rochester?

A. The ore was found in 1912 in this mining camp in Pershing County.

—⊗∞—

Q. On what date did William Talcott discover silver in Pony Canyon, which soon grew into the town of Austin?

A. May 2, 1862.

—⊗∞—

Q. On what date and by whom was silver discovered in Tonopah?

A. May 19, 1900, by Jim and Belle Butler.

—⊗∞—

Q. When and where was Nevada's highest temperature recorded?

A. On June 29, 1994, it reached 125 degrees in Laughlin on the Colorado River.

—⊗∞—

Q. What is the name of one of the world's largest outdoor scientific laboratories?

A. The Nevada Test Site.

—⊗∞—

Q. Established in the early 1950s, what was the primary mission of the test site?

A. The testing of atomic bombs.

—⊗∞—

Q. What was the name of the aircraft designer from Van Nuys, CA, who moved to Las Vegas in 1966 with the dream of establishing a jet plane manufacturing company?

A. John Morgan.

Q. What is the average annual rainfall in Las Vegas?

A. About four inches.

———∞∞———

Q. What was the highest temperature ever recorded in Las Vegas?

A. One hundred seventeen degrees on July 24, 1942.

———∞∞———

Q. When and how long was the record "hot spell" (over 100 degrees) in Las Vegas?

A. Sixty-six days in 1944, from June 27 to August 31.

———∞∞———

Q. What were the highest winds ever recorded at Nellis Air Force Base near Las Vegas?

A. More than 80 miles an hour, on July 18, 1994.

———∞∞———

Q. In what month and what year did the Las Vegas area experience a tornado, a flood, and an earthquake (none of which resulted in major damage)?

A. April 1992.

———∞∞———

Q. During the last decade of the 20th century, what "flights" have taken place over western Nevada without public knowledge?

A. Unarmed missiles fired from Navy ships in the Pacific, targeted to land at specified remote locations.

Q. What two federal installations have been "targets" for these missiles?

A. The Tonopah Test Range and the Fallon Naval Air Station.

———∞∞∞———

Q. Why is most of the town of Austin built on the hill north of U.S. Hwy. 50?

A. To take advantage of the winter sun.

———∞∞∞———

Q. What are the conditions for Austinites who live south of the highway?

A. A hill blocks the sun in wintertime, and they may not see their shadows from November until March.

———∞∞∞———

Q. Who holds the position of state metrologist, and what does he do?

A. Steve Grabski, who makes sure that your supermarket scales are correct and that the gallon of gas you pump at your service station is really one gallon.

———∞∞∞———

Q. Legislation to establish a U.S. Mint at Carson City was passed by both houses of Congress on what date?

A. March 3, 1863 (before Nevada became a state).

———∞∞∞———

Q. In what year did the first six-ton press arrive at the Carson mint?

A. 1869.

Q. On what date was the first coin struck, bearing the soon-to-be-famous "CC" mint mark?

A. February 11, 1870.

Q. What was the production capacity of the press?

A. 1,500 coins per hour.

Q. What was the first coin struck at the Carson City Mint?

A. A seated Liberty silver dollar.

Q. During what years did the Carson City Mint produce coins?

A. From 1870 to 1885, and again from 1889 to 1893.

Q. When did the Carson City Mint cease coining operations?

A. 1893.

Q. What happened to Press No. 1 following closure of the Carson City Mint?

A. It was first moved to the Philadelphia Mint, then in 1945 it was transferred to the San Francisco Mint.

Q. The old press was due to be scrapped in 1955, but it was returned to Carson City for display in the Nevada State Museum in what year?

A. 1958.

Q. How much did the State of Nevada pay for the press as a museum piece?

A. $225.

Q. In 1964 the nation was faced with a severe coin shortage, and the old press was moved to what other mint to again produce coins?

A. The Denver Mint.

Q. During the next three years, how many coins were struck on the old press at the Denver Mint?

A. One hundred eighty-eight million.

Q. In what year was the press again returned to the Carson City Museum?

A. 1967.

Q. The old press was again put into operation in 1976 for what purpose?

A. To strike Nevada Bicentennial medals in gold, silver, copper, and bronze.

Q. What is the current operational status of the old press?

A. Under supervision, visitors to the museum may strike their own bronze medals on specified days during the summer months.

Q. At 1:41 P.M. on December 14, 1998, what "event" rattled some Las Vegans?

A. A 2.7-magnitude earthquake in the northwest area of town.

―――∞∞∞―――

Q. What was the Las Vegas area's most powerful earthquake in recent years?

A. A 3.5-magnitude earthquake in November, 1989, did minor damage in north Las Vegas.

―――∞∞∞―――

Q. Geologists have mapped how many faults in the Las Vegas area?

A. About 20.

―――∞∞∞―――

Q. Which of these faults is considered the most potentially damaging?

A. The Decatur Fault is said to be long enough to cause a 6.5 quake.

―――∞∞∞―――

Q. What Las Vegas not-for-profit group is funded by the U.S. Department of Energy to facilitate commercialization of solar technology in southern Nevada?

A. Corporation for Solar Technology and Renewable Resources (CSTRR).

―――∞∞∞―――

Q. Why is Nevada ideally suited for the study and production of solar energy?

A. Nevada has an average of 85 percent sunny days.

Q. Solar power in Nevada is to reach 1 percent of total by what year?

A. 2009.

──────⊗≫o──────

Q. What is Nevada Power Company's Green Power Program?

A. Customers can add money over and above their monthly power bill to help pay for the power company's development, construction, and marketing of solar power.

──────⊗≫o──────

Q. What percent of Nevadans surveyed "have an interest in" using solar power, even if it costs more than power generated by other means?

A. Eighty-four percent.

──────⊗≫o──────

Q. How many solar technologies are being studied or used in Nevada?

A. Four.

──────⊗≫o──────

Q. What are the four solar technologies?

A. Photovoltaic, solar power towers, dish stirling systems, and solar parabolic trough collectors.

──────⊗≫o──────

Q. What is the name of the largest scientific research laboratory at the University of Nevada, Las Vegas?

A. The Harry Reid Center for Environmental Studies (HRC).

Q. What is the size and location of the Nevada Test Site?

A. 1,350 square miles, about 70 miles northwest of Las Vegas.

Q. What are the names of the three major valleys in the Test Site?

A. Yucca Flat, Frenchman Flat, and Jackass Flat.

Q. What was the name of this atomic testing site when it was first established?

A. The Nevada Proving Grounds (NPG).

Q. The NPG was established on what date by what U.S. president?

A. January 11, 1951, by President Harry S. Truman.

Q. On what date was the first atmospheric atomic detonation at the NPG?

A. January 27, 1951.

Q. What was the name, size, and location of this first atomic test?

A. Able, a one-kiloton device, was detonated 1,060 feet above the surface of Frenchman Flat.

Q. The first five detonations, part of the Operation Ranger series, were dropped from what?

A. B-50 bombers that flew out of Kirtland AFB in Albuquerque, NM.

Q. What detonation at the NPG broke several store windows in Las Vegas?

A. Baker-2, an eight-kiloton device tested on February 2, 1951.

———— ∞ ————

Q. When was a post office opened at Mercury, the base camp for the NPG?

A. March 1, 1952.

———— ∞ ————

Q. In what ways were atomic devices tested at the Nevada Test Site?

A. Air-drop, tower, surface, tunnel, and balloon tests.

———— ∞ ————

Q. From 1951 to 1962, how many atmospheric tests were conducted at the NTS?

A. One hundred.

———— ∞ ————

Q. What agency of the federal government built the Nevada Test Site?

A. The Atomic Energy Commission.

———— ∞ ————

Q. A typical small community built near ground zero was destroyed by what test?

A. Annie (named Shamrock by the press) was fired March 17, 1953.

———— ∞ ————

Q. Which U.S. president declared a moratorium on all nuclear testing, and when?

A. President Dwight D. Eisenhower stopped all testing on October 31, 1958.

Q. Underground testing was resumed at the NTS on what date?

A. September 15, 1961.

———∞———

Q. How many atomic tests were conducted at the NTS during 1962?

A. Sixty-two.

———∞———

Q. What was the name and date of the last airdrop atomic test at the NTS?

A. The last HA (High Altitude) test was conducted April 6, 1955.

———∞———

Q. Why is the Grable, a 15-kiloton shot at the NTS on May 25, 1953, significant?

A. It was the only time a nuclear artillery shell was ever fired.

———∞———

Q. By the end of 1993, how many nuclear tests had been conducted at the NTS?

A. Nine hundred twenty-five.

———∞———

Q. When was a balloon first used as a detonation platform at the NTS?

A. June 5, 1957.

———∞———

Q. How tall were the test towers built at the NTS for nuclear detonations?

A. As high as 700 feet.

Q. What was the Plowshare Program at the NTS on March 12, 1968?

A. A simultaneous detonation of five 1.1-kiloton devices in a row.

Q. When was Camp Desert Rock activated at the NTS, and for what purpose?

A. To house as many as 6,000 troops during military maneuvers.

Q. What was the name given to the hill from which the press observed nuclear tests at NTS?

A. News Nob.

Q. What was the name of the second nationally televised nuclear test at the NTS?

A. Apple II, detonated from a 500-foot tower on May 5, 1955.

Q. This test, which destroyed cars, houses, and mannequins, was conducted by what federal agency?

A. The Federal Civil Defense Administration.

Q. Why did Civil Defense conduct this test?

A. To assess the impacts of nuclear detonations on civilian populations.

Q. What was the purpose of the Sedan test at the NTS on July 6, 1962?

A. To develop technology to use nuclear energy for earth moving projects.

———⊗⊗⊗———

Q. How large was the Sedan device, and where was it detonated?

A. Sedan was a 104-kiloton device detonated 635 feet underground.

———⊗⊗⊗———

Q. How large was the crater made by the Sedan test?

A. 1,280 feet in diameter and 320 feet deep.

———⊗⊗⊗———

Q. What was Project Pluto at the NTS?

A. A large, costly, and complex program begun in 1957 to create a nuclear ramjet engine.

———⊗⊗⊗———

Q. Was a nuclear ramjet engine ever built and tested at the NTS?

A. Yes, on May 14, 1961, the engine sitting on a railroad flat car roared to life for a few seconds.

———⊗⊗⊗———

Q. Who sponsored Project Pluto, and what came of it?

A. Sponsored by the Pentagon, the project was canceled on July 1, 1964, seven and one-half years after it was "born."

———⊗⊗⊗———

Q. What were the Air Force Peacekeeper experiments at the NTS?

A. Building and testing facilities for the MX missile.

Q. How big was the hole dug to be used as a concrete silo for the MX?

A. Eighteen feet in diameter, 130 feet deep.

Q. What is the name of the mountain in Nevada where the longest, most costly, and most hotly debated scientific studies in the history of nuclear energy are being conducted?

A. Yucca Mountain.

Q. Yucca Mountain is the proposed site for what?

A. Permanent storage of high-level nuclear waste.

Q. In what year did the Yucca Mountain studies begin?

A. 1976.

Q. In what year did Congress pass the Nuclear Waste Policy Act?

A. 1982.

Q. When did Congress amend the nuclear waste act and direct the DOE to study only Yucca Mountain for permanent high-level waste storage?

A. December 1987.

Q. The Nuclear Waste Fund established by Congress did what?

A. Required people who use electrical power from nuclear plants pay into this fund through their power bills.

Q. How many electrical generating plants in Nevada operate by nuclear power?

A. None.

———∞∞∞———

Q. What is the Exploratory Studies Facility at Yucca Mountain?

A. A 14-mile loop of tunnels to house laboratories and test facilities.

———∞∞∞———

Q. How deep below the mountain ridge is the ESF located?

A. 1,000 feet.

———∞∞∞———

Q. What event occurred June 29, 1992, that revived concerns about the site?

A. A 5.6-magnitude earthquake 12 miles from Yucca Mountain.

———∞∞∞———

Q. A dust storm forced what famed woman pilot to land at what Nevada airport?

A. In the early 1930s, Amelia Earhart set down at the Lovelock airfield.

———∞∞∞———

Q. What type of plane was Earhart piloting?

A. An experimental autogiro.

———∞∞∞———

Q. What are the geological features at Ash Meadows?

A. Spring-fed wetlands and alkaline desert uplands.

Q. How many species of plants and animals at Ash Meadows are found nowhere else in the world?

A. Twenty-four.

⸺⸱⸺

Q. What product from what official state tree has been used commercially and spiritually since prerecorded history?

A. The pinyon pine nuts, or seeds.

⸺⸱⸺

Q. In what months of the year are the pinyon pine nuts harvested?

A. September and October.

⸺⸱⸺

Q. The pinyon pine trees grow where in Nevada?

A. At the higher elevations over the state.

⸺⸱⸺

Q. How long does Mother Nature require for the seeds to mature?

A. Two years.

⸺⸱⸺

Q. How many months of the year has snowfall been recorded at Great Basin National Park?

A. Twelve.

⸺⸱⸺

Q. In what year did Southern California Edison acquire 2,500 acres for construction of a coal-fed power plant near Laughlin?

A. 1966, the same year the town of Laughlin was founded.